Endorsements:

"Terra Bundance is a wellspring of knowledge providing you with tips, tools, and techniques to unleash you from your past to soar like a butterfly into your future. Tapping into ancient and new wisdom, Terra guides you from limiting beliefs and moves with you into new thought patterns of love, freedom and your ultimate purpose. Having this book in your hands is like having your very own Transformational guru."

~Jen Moore, M.S., B.A. Feminist Activist, Scholar, Researcher, Teacher, Author

"Terra taps into the Infinite Wisdom of the Ages and brings forth a clear message of Love and Transformation."

~Rev. Shannon O'Hurley, Associate Minister, New Thought Center for Spiritual Living, *newthoughtcsl.org*

"Some books are just read, and others are meant to be experienced. The Butterfly Process is one such workbook… a unique experience in a world of sameness. At a time when so many are fed up with feeding the mind, Terra Bundance does everything possible (and then some!) to get you into your body, to make deep transformative changes, and not just read the same concepts over and over in slightly different words from different authors. The concepts are logical, and the ideas well thought out. Also, unlike many books, if you can't do it on your own, this book is a veritable encyclopedia of resources to further your process. Terra stands with and upon the shoulders of the greats and puts it all into one copious, attainable package."

~Dave Markowitz, Medical Intuitive, Spiritual Healer, Author, *davemarkowitz.com*

"This perfectly wrapped gift of pages is evidence that Terra Bundance knows in a deep way that the Infinite Heart longs to have YOUR unique colors and lucid wings soaring through Her shimmering skies"

~Ash Ruiz, Musician/Spiritual Teacher, *ashruiz.com*

The Butterfly Process
Tools For Transformation

Terra Bundance

The Butterfly Process: Tools for Transformation

All rights reserved,
COPYRIGHT© 2014 by Terra Bundance

Editors:
    Holly Wells, *hollyw25@comcast.net*
    Lori Rising, *www.authorshipforexperts.com*

Editing Team:
    Michael Doss, *shineyourlifellc@gmail.com*
    Alison Hilber, *spiritualmigrations.com*
    Lama Thubten, *lamathubten@gmail.com / thubten.me*

Design Team:
    Cover Design - Garrett Purchio, *garrettpurchio@gmail.com*
    Interior Design – Adrian Emery, *emerypagedesign@gmail.com*

Cover Art and Internal Artwork

Various artists created the artwork and poetry throughout this book. See pp. 135 & 136 for contact information for each of them. All artwork is copyrighted and owned by Terra Bundance or the artist, and cannot be used without written permission.

Supported by:
- Author Paradise, *authorparadise.com*
- New Thought Center for Spiritual Living, Lake Oswego, Oregon, *newthoughtcsl.org*
- Luminary Voices, *luminaryvoices.com*

This book may not be reproduced in whole or in part without written permission from the author, except by a reviewer who may quote brief passages in a review; no part of this book may be reproduced, stored in a retrieval system, or transmitted in any form or by any means (electronic, mechanical, photocopying, recording, or other) without written permission from the author.

Table of Contents

p. 1 Endorsements
p. 2 Title Page
p. 3 Copyright, Editor, and Support Information
p. 4 Table of Contents

p. 6 **Preliminaries**
p. 6 Author Information
p. 7 Thanks
p. 8 Dedication & Disclaimer
p. 9 Introduction: Learning to Fly
p. 12 Poem: "Fly!"
p. 13 Get the Most from This Book
p. 14 The Butterfly Process Summary
p. 15 What is *The Butterfly Process*?
p. 17 Why the Butterfly?
p. 19 Chakras and *The Butterfly Process*

p. 22 **I. The Egg Stage**
p. 22 Main Focus: Choosing and Nurturing Change
p. 23 Chakras for The Egg Stage
p. 24 Egg Check-In: Am I Ready?
p. 26 Embrace The Egg: Be Here
p. 27 Affirmation for The Egg Stage
p. 28 Tools for The Egg Stage
p. 52 Egg Conclusion: Embrace Change, Nurture Yourself
p. 54 Journal Section for The Egg Stage

p. 58 **II. The Caterpillar Stage**
p. 58 Main Focus: Transformation and Paying Attention
p. 60 Chakras for The Caterpillar Stage
p. 60 Caterpillar Check-In: Am I Willing?
p. 61 Embrace The Caterpillar: Open Yourself to Transform
p. 62 Affirmation for The Caterpillar Stage
p. 62 Tools for The Caterpillar Stage

p. 77 Caterpillar Conclusion: Try New Things, Pay Attention
p. 79 Journal Section for The Caterpillar Stage

p. 84 **III. The Cocoon Stage**
p. 84 Main Focus: Nurturing Integration
p. 86 Chakras for The Cocoon Stage
p. 86 Cocoon Stage Check-In: Am I Capable?
p. 87 Embrace The Cocoon: Focus Fully
p. 89 Affirmation for The Cocoon Stage
p. 89 Tools for The Cocoon Stage
p. 102 Cocoon Conclusion: Be Quiet and Reflect
p. 103 Journal Section for The Cocoon Stage

p. 108 **IV. The Butterfly Stage**
p. 108 Main Focus: Presence and Integrity
p. 109 Chakras for The Butterfly Stage
p. 110 Butterfly Check-In: Taking Responsibility!
p. 113 Embrace The Butterfly: Honesty & Authenticity
p. 115 Affirmation for The Butterfly Stage
p. 115 Tools for The Butterfly Stage
p. 128 Butterfly Conclusion: Live in the Present
p. 129 Journal section for The Butterfly Stage

p. 133 *The Butterfly Process* Conclusion
p. 134 Postscript
p. 135 Artists and Poets
p. 137 Explanation of Terms
p. 139 Toolbox Summary
p. 143 Main Journal

Preliminaries:
About the Author

Terra Bundance lives in Portland, Oregon with her Beloved, Michael Doss and their new baby boy; dogs, Lucy and Buddy; cat, Moo; and, part-time, with Michael's four beautiful children.

Terra is a Cheerleader for Oneness, Empathic Intuitive, and Vocal Empowerment Coach. She creates Transformation Tools such as books, music, meditations, raw chocolate, Kombucha and more; she performs, sings, speaks, teaches, motivates, inspires and co-creates with other conscious people.

To contact Terra, find more of her Transformation Tools, read her *Terra Out Loud* blog or find out where she will be speaking and/or performing, go to: *terrabundance.com*.

Special Thanks

To my Beloved, *Michael Doss*, for being my partner, my love, my mirror, my biggest fan, an ever present, patient, loving support in my life, my very first editor, father to our baby boy, and my personal "Guru of Trust." I love you so, my Beloved!

To my MamaDiddy, *Bill and Sherry Farmer*, for being my very FIRST biggest fans, (even before I was born), for always loving and supporting me no matter how hard it might have been, and for always holding my best and highest good for me even when I may have forgotten it for myself. I chose the best parents possible!

To my Soul Sisters, *Amy M.*, *Charlotte S.*, *Jen M.*, *JJ H.*, *Stasia B.*, *Laura B.*, *Amy S.*, and *Elora D.*, thank you for being my most amazing, beautiful, constant reflections, for reminding me to remain ever present, for learning and growing with me, and for *"Authentically Being There"* with and for me.

To two of my Soul Brothers, *Dylan S.* and *Brad B.*, thank you for the constant loving support you have each given me! From the editing help to the hugs, and for always cheering me on my path, deep gratitude and love to you both.

To my dear friend, spiritual mentor, and author-guru support, *Susan Buckley*, gratitude is not a big enough word for how much I appreciate and honor the experience of you in my life. You are so very important to me. I can only say thank you, and continue to show you the love and support that I always feel from you.

To my many AWESOME Soul Sisters and Brothers (so many to name ... and you know who you are!) for your patience, support, love, and guidance as I have learned, used, and practiced all of the many tools in this book with you. You have taught me so much. This book would not have happened without each and every one of you.

And to my amazing editor, *Holly Wells*, who walked through deep cleansing, release, acceptance, and growth with me to help make this book come to life. You are so amazing! What a gift you are to me.

THANK YOU ALL so much for always showing up as my best teachers, and for supporting and pushing me to breathe life into this, my very first book! *I love you!*

Dedication

I dedicate this book to my brother,
Tyson Farmer

I don't think I would have finished this book if I had not realized just how much I truly care about and love you. Tyson, I am *so blessed* to be your sister. I have and always will learn so much from you, even from thousands of miles away! Thank you for continually growing up with me through our childhood and our lives. I love you brother!

> **Disclaimer:** *The information in this book is intended for educational purposes only. It is not the intention of Terra Bundance or her affiliates to advise on emotional, mental, or physical health care. Terra Bundance is not a licensed medical professional, counselor, or therapist. This book is based on her personal work, study, reading, learning, and experiences, and was written for the sole purpose of offering this information to you, the reader, to use as you see fit. You have the choice to seek professional help for any personal, physical, mental, or emotional concerns you may have. The information here is not intended to prevent, diagnose, treat, or cure any disease.*

Introduction:
Learning to Fly

"I can feel myself outgrowing this life I've been living in."
~ *"Butterfly" song by Jana Stanfield*

I love to support people through transformation. It is one of the most important things I feel I am here to do. I have been saving my personal tools and inner guidance about change and transformation in journals for many years, planning to "possibly" share some of them with my friends and family one day. Then suddenly, this book came to life!

The Butterfly Process is the name I have given to a process I use in pretty much every new experience I move through in my life. I have discovered that when I can be quiet and notice *where* I am in the process, I am able to bring more clarity and awareness to any situation. I can then seek and allow various forms of support as I move through one stage to the next. *The Butterfly Process* has helped me become more patient, present, kind, and gentle with my loved ones and myself. It supports me in taking responsibility, and helps me to not blame others when I feel stuck. It allows me to be more available in every aspect of my life.

I have found that once I use *The Butterfly Process* to work through some major "issue" in my life, I generally do not have to revisit the same issue again. And if the issue does "reappear," I am in a more advanced stage of awareness so that clearing the *next* level is much easier and gentler than the original experience. That being said, I will not mince words. You will move through your "stuff" as you use *The Butterfly Process*.

Take a few deep breaths and decide in *this* moment if you are willing to face fears that may have held you back in your life. Think about why you might have picked up this book. While you breathe deeply and contemplate letting go of that which no longer serves you, give yourself permission to feel any anxiety, fears, nervousness, excitement, or other emotions that may come up.

If you are "sick and tired of being sick and tired," you are ready to step into this process. If you have been calling something into your life to support internal change in a gentle way, then you are ready for this process. If you have been saying to the people in your life that you are just done with "being unhappy," or "not fitting in," or "feeling stuck," or "not finding your purpose," then you may have come to just the right place.

Please consider that you are *always* heard. You are *always* supported. You are *always* and in-all-ways *One with Divine Guidance*. NOW is the time to step into your most empowered Divine Self and to allow yourself to be guided and supported. When you take on this process, you are saying YES to change. You are saying, "I am ready to find my true voice and to step more fully into my purpose and my passion!"

I know this book, the process, and the toolboxes have the capacity to support you on all levels as you step onto and embrace the path of your purpose and passion.

The Butterfly Process is a workbook, a self-help book, a journal, a resource, and a reference book. Whether you create your own tools or adopt someone else's, you are always building your own personal "toolbox for transformation." Since change is considered the only true constant (other than love), you are likely to be moving through some form of transformation or change at all times. After you go through

The Butterfly Process the first time, it is easy to use it again and again for guidance, references and reminders, as well as for any new issues that may arise.

It requires courage and strength to step onto the path of your personal "journey on purpose." By taking care of yourself, you become a much better partner, parent, employee, friend, YOU! Congratulations, blessings, and love to you on your sacred transformational journey!

I would like to add that I have not been approached by, nor am I endorsed by any of the tools, recommendations, suggestions or people I mention throughout this book. Everything I have written is based on my own personal experience and research, or things I have created on my own.

Terra Bundance

Clackamas, OR

P.S. My very favorite affirmation is one I learned at my Spiritual Home, *New Thought Center for Spiritual Living* (NTCSL) in Lake Oswego, Oregon. This is a slightly adapted version of the Affirmation Statement our entire congregation says before every Sunday morning service, and I share it here in the knowing that it can support you too. Blessings!

> *I am open and receptive as I receive this message today.*
> *Something I am about to hear (read) applies to my life.*
> *I am here by Divine appointment to receive spiritual tools*
> *for personal transformation, and to help make the world a*
> *better place. My life's purpose is already within me, and I*
> *am committed to its unfoldment.*
> *As I hear (read) truth today, I am set free.*

Fly!

Tears of pain shot through her delicate body as she grew and the cocoon tightened around her. She fought moment by moment to catch her breath and find comfort. She knew that these final truths spoken were tightly wrapped around her and provided the needed struggle for her to build strength. Her prayer affirmed her greatest desire for freedom of expression. She screamed out in ecstatic form and claimed the highest vision for her life; it was time for her to fly.

~Christine Ruddy

Get the MOST from this book!

1) Use *colored pencils, crayons, or markers* instead of a pen or pencil when you are writing, creating, or drawing.

2) *Color the images* as you make your way through the book.

3) *Draw special "tools"* into the toolboxes for each stage. (pp. 28, 62, 89, and 115)

4) Be sure to read the **Postscript** (p. 134) and *Artists' Information* (pp. 135-136).

5) Find *explanations* for some terms (p. 137).

6) *Add your own tool ideas* to the toolbox summary at the end of the book (pp. 139-142).

7) Use the *Journal pages* located at the end of each stage, (pp. 54, 79, 103, and 129) and at the end of the book (pp. 143-164) to record your own ideas, notes, thoughts, and creations.

8) *"Self" Check-in*- If at ANY point while reading this book you feel anxious, stressed, like you are taking in too much information, or you simply need a break, put down the book and try one or more of the following:

Walk barefoot on Mama Earth, drink water, take deep breaths, take a nap, journal, talk to someone you trust, use some essential oils, lie in the sun, listen to peaceful music, or do something that you love and that grounds you.

The Butterfly Process:
A Summary

There are 4 stages to this process.

In each stage, this book will help you-

❖ *Discover many new tools to add to your own personal Toolbox*

❖ *Practice being present in each of the Stages you find yourself in.*

❖ *Gain helpful information on how to learn from the suggestions and tools in each stage.*

❖ *Create tools of your own to learn how to support yourself through change.*

You will be:

❖ Guided through meditations.

❖ Asked to answer questions.

❖ Given tasks and journaling suggestions.

❖ Encouraged to be honest with yourself.

The main purpose of *The Butterfly Process* is to get you *out of* suffering and victimhood on ALL levels and *into* claiming your Bliss at all times.

What is the Butterfly Process?

"There's an old saying that nothing is permanent but change. When we are open to it, we can learn and grow through all types of changes. Change offers newfound freedom... when we realize that, we are secure in knowing that change is good, and good for us."
~Lissa Coffey

Life Cycle of a Butterfly

Wherever you may be in your life, you are moving through some form of transformation, change, evolution or growth. If you are feeling challenged by your life experiences, are ready to fully allow the experience of letting go of what no longer supports you, and are ready to allow your healing to begin, you are ready to engage yourself in *The Butterfly Process*.

Whether you like to admit it or not, you are almost always moving through some phase of change in your life. *It is up to you* to decide if you are willing to face whatever emotional or spiritual challenges that change generally brings, or become overwhelmed and paralyzed by them. It is possible to heal old patterns, wounds, or *pain-bodies* (Terms p. 137) that are likely to come up during change. *The Butterfly Process* can guide and support you through your experience.

You may exhibit some new, strange, different, or unexplainable emotions and patterns as you move through this book—which is likely to be a tangible sign of healing. Because of this, you also may require support from friends, family, partners, therapists, healers, teachers, spiritual practitioners, life coaches, or others. I strongly suggest you seek whatever support you can, and allow it to help you as you step onto this path of transformation. At least consider discussing that you are clearing some old patterns with someone close to you. Change can often feel lonely. It's nice to know you are supported when you choose to embark on a journey of transformation.

The "toolbox" of support you are creating for use throughout your life will be filled with an amazing assortment of useful tools as you learn to move through any old fear, "stuckness," suffering, *pain-bodies*, or ego-voices that may be intent on forcing you to relive old patterns that keep you frustrated and unfulfilled.

Be fully present with where you are, and move through this process *in the time you need* instead of plowing through it. If you push yourself too much you may miss some of the most important, small details that will inevitably show up at another time in your life to be cleared.

Any time I feel uncomfortable and need to create a safe environment for myself, one of my favorite things to do is sing. Below is a chant I created to share as you begin your journey. You may wish to repeat this chant, or another of your choosing, as many times as necessary as you step onto the path of your new life: *"All my spirits, all my relations, I welcome you. Teach me my truth."* You can also listen to this chant on the terrabundance.com Music page.

Why the Butterfly?

The butterfly has long been a symbol of change, transformation, transmutation, and evolution. It is also a symbol for elegance, beauty, and grace. Perhaps, most significantly, the butterfly teaches us **the art of letting go**.

The butterfly has greatly impressed itself on us in many ways. This graceful, small creature has so much significance in many cultures of our world!

- The butterfly is very fragile and can even die if handled incorrectly, and yet, monarch families are known to migrate (yes, fly!) over 3,000 MILES!
- Butterflies are used as the image for a powerful metaphor known as "The Butterfly Effect" or Chaos Theory:

    "The phenomenon whereby a small change at one place in a complex system can have large effects elsewhere" (thefreedictionary.com).

    From the original chaos theory on predicting weather: *"A butterfly flapping its wings in South America can affect the weather in Central Park"* (~ Edward Lorenz, creator of the Chaos Theory).

- Butterflies are beautiful and inspiring in their gracefulness and have been the muse for many artists, authors, poets, musicians, movies, and more. Such a tiny creature given so much prestige!
- From one of my favorite books: *"Probably no animal or insect has come to represent the process of transformation and shape-shifting more than the butterfly"* (*Animal Speak* by Ted Andrews, p. 339)

There seems no simpler way to define or describe the process of embracing change than to describe the life of a butterfly. I personally believe that if humans embraced transformation, change, and evolution as easily as the butterfly, many of the stresses of the world could be dissolved more peacefully and gracefully.

The butterfly starts off as an egg, hatches alone, feeds itself, grows as a caterpillar, fixes itself to a leaf or branch, forms a cocoon, mutates, becomes liquid, grows an entirely new body including wings, opens its cocoon alone, waits patiently for its new wings to strengthen, open and dry, and then, it flies! It never questions its meaning. It just lets go and moves to the next thing, not even knowing what that might be. That is the quintessential "Art of Letting Go"! Each step brings this tiny being closer to its magnificent destiny. The butterfly starts off as a dot on a leaf, and ends up with glorious wings… and it FLIES! We as humans can learn so much from the butterfly's life.

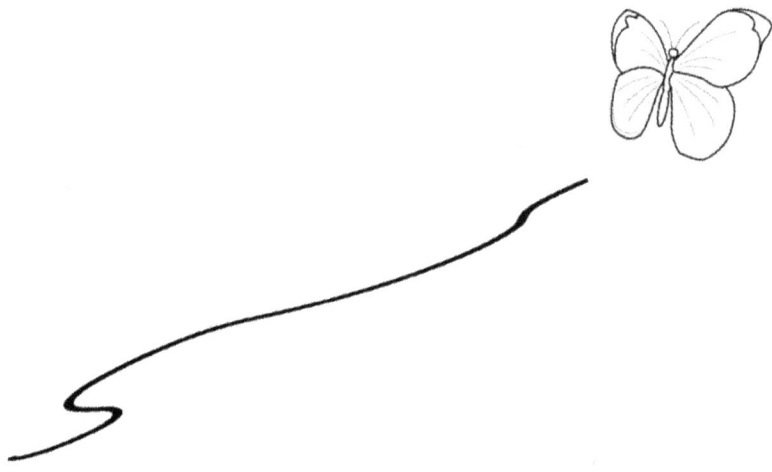

Chakras and The Butterfly Process:

Another form of support you may choose to use while journeying through this book is the chakra system of the body's energy field. Many people consider where they are in life as correlating with one of seven main chakras. On the next two pages I have added two charts to offer an idea of which chakras you are likely to be working with during each stage of The Butterfly Process.

A general definition of chakra is, *"Seven energy centers aligned from the base of the spine to the top of the head. The chakras are part of the subtle body, meaning that they are not anatomical in nature. The Sanskrit term comes from the word for wheel and the chakras are often thought of as spinning wheels of energy. It is believed that when all the chakras are in alignment, your life force (kundalini) can travel up the spine to the crown of the head. When the chakras get blocked, it prevents one from reaching an enlightened state"* (*yoga.about.com*).

Please take note: each person is different, and each may feel it differently from what I am suggesting here. The following is a basic reference or guide for those of you who are new to chakra work or those who might simply be curious.

For more information about chakras, go to any of the following sites and search "chakra": *yoga.about.com; healing.about.com; chopra.com; chakraenergy.com*

The image below depicts the general location and basic names of the seven main chakras:

(I have also included the high-heart chakra and call it Chakra 4½. I work with the high-heart chakra often. I discuss it in this book, and feel it is important to add here.)

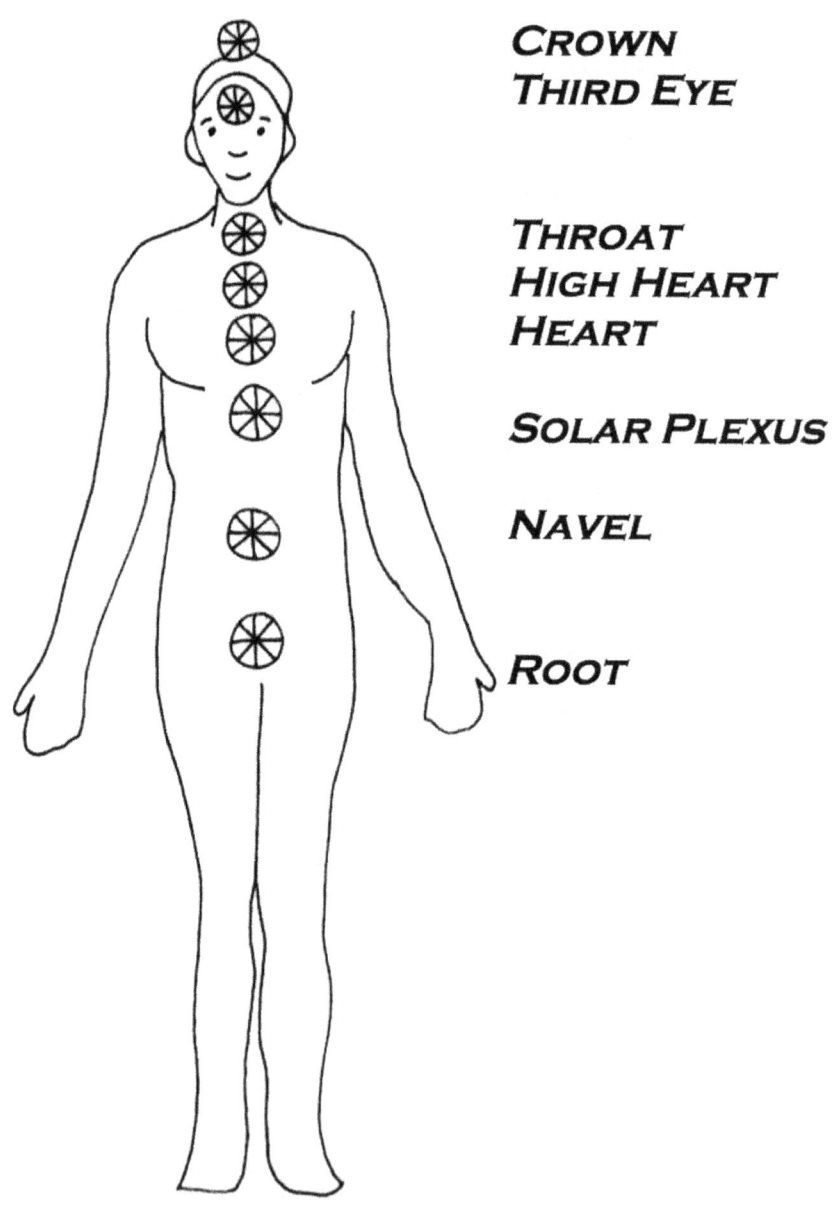

Chakras and The Butterfly Process

*Each chakra generally corresponds with a color,
which I added next to the chakra name*

* **Chakras 1, 2, 3**   Egg Stage
    1) Root/Red   Chakra info- p. 23
    2) Navel/Orange
    3) Solar Plexus/Yellow

* **Chakras 4, 4½ , 5**   Caterpillar Stage
    4) Heart/Green   Chakra info- p. 60
    4½) High Heart/Turquoise or Pink
    5) Throat/Light or Bright Blue

* **Chakras 6, 7**   Cocoon Stage
    6) Third Eye/Indigo   Chakra info- p. 86
    7) Crown/Violet or White

* **ALL of the Chakras**   Butterfly Stage
    1) Root/Red   Chakra info- p. 109
    2) Navel/Orange
    3) Solar Plexus/Yellow
    4) Heart/Green
    4½) High Heart/Turquoise or Pink
    5) Throat/Light or Bright Blue
    6) Third Eye/Indigo
    7) Crown/Violet or White

I. The Egg Stage

"The beginning is the most important part of the work."
~Plato

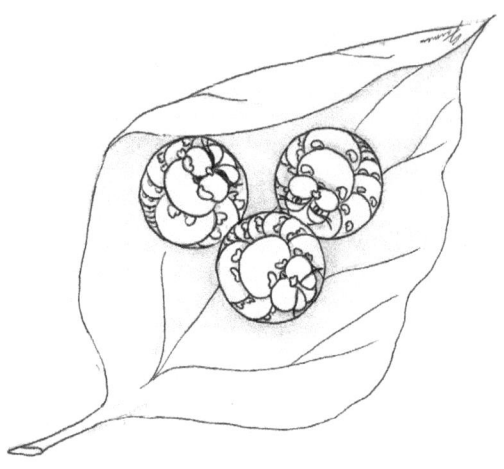

In the Egg Stage, you are starting something new, noticing a change or shift beginning, feeling something different, intrigued and possibly uncomfortable with the idea of change. This is a time to open up to transforming your life.

Egg Stage Main Focus:
Choosing and Nurturing Change

This is the stage where you decide, "**It is time for a change, and I have a choice to embrace the change.**" This can be a very fragile stage. Much like the beginning of any life, this is a place where you may be quite vulnerable. This stage tends to be the most difficult to step into because the ego wants to hold on to comfort-zones, and safe, easy, less-challenging experiences. Another thing the ego likes to do is to jump quickly past any emotions that might come up, and skip the parts that feel like struggle or work. When this happens, there is usually a constant revisiting of the old emotions and patterns. This can often lead to one or more of the following: major anxiety, sickness, depression, mood swings, panic, anger, rage, hiding from life, addictions, or constantly changing jobs, relationships, homes, or friends.

Without conscious awareness, the Egg Stage (or even *pre*-Egg Stage) is where many people remain stuck until some major health problem happens, an emotional breakdown occurs, or some devastating past memory comes to the surface. Often, only when this breakdown occurs do people finally choose to seek medical attention or therapy, or, sadly, become caught up in addictive experiences or behavior like drugs, alcohol, excessive exercise, work, food, sex, or abusive relationships or situations to avoid dealing with the issues. By consciously entering into the Egg Stage, you are *making the choice to change* and *to start taking responsibility* for your life.

Chakras for the Egg Stage

In this stage, you are working with the 1st (Root/Red), 2nd (Navel/Orange), and 3rd (Solar Plexus/Yellow) chakras, which are all about your connection to the physical world and your body, the beliefs you have created and lived by up to this point, and how your basic instincts have expressed as a result of those beliefs. They are also the chakras that house your own personal functional patterns and connections to being alive in the world; plus, your patterns around family, friends, and relationships.

The patterns and habits created in the first three chakras can be somewhat difficult to break, since you have created your life up to this point out of those beliefs, or they were passed down to you through family lines. Once you shift the patterns in the first three chakras, it can become much easier to shift the rest of them.

Egg Stage Check-In:
Am I Ready?

One way to decide if it is time for you to step into the Egg Stage (hopefully *before* some crisis forces you to figure it out) is to sit quietly and breathe deeply (you may wish to use the Heart-Centered Breathing Exercise described on p. 30). Check in with your *inner guidance* (Terms p. 137), tune into your thoughts, feelings and physical body, and do the first exercise below.

Become aware of one issue or situation that has been creating any feelings of stress, worry, anxiety, depression or stuckness in your life. *This is not a time to try to fix anything, just to become* aware *of it.*

First Exercise:

If you wish, take the time to write down your answers in a journal or notebook, in the journal pages available at the end of this section (p. 54), or at the back of this book (p. 143).

Step 1: Find a quiet place to sit. Take a few deep breaths. While focusing on your breathing, ask yourself: *What am I feeling stuck about? Am I worried, anxious, in fear, or depressed? How long have I had this/these feeling(s), thought(s), or physical experience(s)?*

Whatever your answers, note them and move on to the next step. Even if you do not know the full answer, write what you can. Do not think about this too much. The first thought is usually the best one to write down.

Step 2: Ask yourself: *Is this something I have felt, experienced, or thought before?*

Note your response and move to Step 3.

Step 3: Check in with your breathing. Decide if you are still having the same thoughts, physical sensations, or feelings you started with. As you continue, notice if these shift at all.

Note any changes and move on to step 4.

Step 4: Ask yourself: *Is this something I am afraid to talk about or deal with?*

Again, write down your thoughts.

Once you have breathed through this exercise and noted your responses, ask yourself if you are ready to look more deeply at the feelings, thoughts, and emotions that have come to the surface. If you feel ready, move on to the second exercise. If you do not feel ready, or if you have difficulty determining a specific "stuckness," then give yourself some time, talk to a friend or support person, and come back to this when you are ready.

Second Exercise:

Ask yourself the following questions and note your answers:

1) Is this issue something I am consciously allowing myself to be truly and fully present with for the first time?

2) Is this issue something I previously avoided dealing with?

3) Do I have a desire to "ignore" what is coming up, or to simply move into another phase of my life without addressing my feelings?

4) Have I been feeling in any way irritable, moody, unstable, disconnected, emotional, anxious, or depressed?

5) Does it seem like, "I can't shake the feeling that I am 'missing something'?"

6) Have I been afraid to talk to someone about the feelings and emotions that have been coming up?

7) Am I judgmental or critical of myself and/or others?

8) Do I often point out the problems of others and tell them how they can fix or work through their problems?

9) Do I notice that when others ask me how I am doing, I answer briefly, negatively or sarcastically (perhaps with a fake smile), I change the subject, or I avoid the question altogether?

10) Am I worried or concerned about others' judgments or opinions of me?

11) Do I tend to stress over small things and then get mad at myself later for getting so easily frustrated?

If the answer to at least two of the above questions is yes (or even a vague "maybe"), then you are probably ready to step into the Egg Stage. It is time to release some *pain-body* (Terms p. 137) and ego attachment(s), to look at what you have been avoiding, and to embrace something new for your life. Congratulations! You are ready to begin claiming your Empowered Self!

Take a moment to let this sink in. Note any feelings, emotions, concerns, or body responses. Take some time to breathe into whatever comes up before moving to the next section. Take some time to write in your personal journal or this book about what you are feeling and sensing.

Embrace the Egg Stage:

Now that you have established that you are in the Egg Stage, the most important thing you can do right now is **be here**. In other words, do not try to change or escape from anything you may begin to experience.

A natural human response toward change is to avoid any strong feelings and emotions that might come up (even the positive ones) by running away, hiding, or avoiding them altogether. The ego often urges us to remain in comfortable patterns (comfort zones) in our relationships, jobs, and living situations.

However, the main reason to move through *The Butterfly Process* is to get you *out* of suffering and *into* your Bliss. Staying in *any* comfort zone is only "safe" in limited ways and for a short while. Staying "safe" often results in a mundane experience of living that can build, or increase, pain and suffering. After a while, boredom, sickness, frustration, resentment, or hunger for something new is likely to surface.

"Doing the same thing over and over again hoping for different results is the definition of insanity."
~Albert Einstein

(I would add, it is also the definition of suffering.)

This is definitely a time to *consider seeking support* from a therapist, a spiritual teacher, leader, or practitioner, and very close friends you know you can trust. It can also help to *pay attention* to any supportive coincidences or synchronicities that may occur. The more you notice them, the more they can support and guide you.

As you work through this stage, some deeply held emotions might surface: you may find you become irritable, emotional, easy to anger or fall into tears; your thoughts may become chaotic or erratic; you might feel like nobody would understand if you talked about what you are feeling; and you may even wish to avoid attention for fear you will be judged or criticized.

> **NOTE:** *The **utmost patience** is required throughout the Egg Stage. Trying to move through this stage too quickly (possibly avoiding or missing something) is a sign of the ego hoping to avoid your most deeply held emotions, and could result in your having to revisit this issue again later (whether you want to or not).*
>
> *I <u>highly</u> recommend you take your time and pay attention through this stage. When you do, you will likely move through the rest of the stages more clearly, gently, and easily.*

Affirmation for the Egg Stage:

Breathe in and out from your heart and say to yourself out loud:

"I am open to creating a place within me for new experiences in my life. I am now willing to release any patterns that no longer serve me and to embrace new ways to support my personal and spiritual growth."

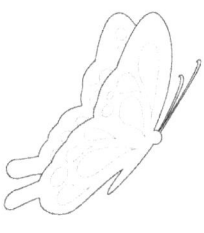

Tools for the Egg Stage:

- *Notes for this stage can be made in the Egg Stage Journal pp. 54-57, or the Main Journal pp. 143-164.*
- *You can add your own tools for this stage on p. 139.*
- *Draw "Tools" to go into your toolbox below.*
- *Creative suggestion: Gift yourself with a new journal to use throughout this book.*

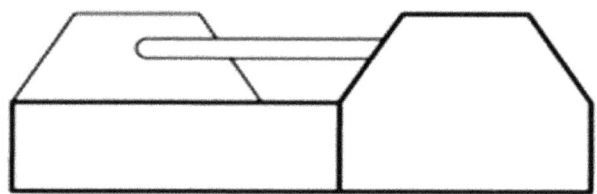

1) Take Responsibility (p. 29)
2) Heart-Centered Breathing (p. 30)
3) Journaling (p. 31)
4) Emotional Freedom Technique (EFT) (p. 33)
5) The Corral Exercise (p. 34)
6) Cleansing/Clearing Baths or Showers (p. 45)
7) Meditation (p. 46)
8) Yoga (p. 47)
9) Supportive Groups and Individuals (p. 48)
10) Your Intention for Food, Water and Other Life-Energy (p. 49)
11) Acceptance (p. 50)
12) Gratitude (p. 51)
13) Creating Your Own Tools (p. 52)

Below are descriptions of The Egg Stage Tools, *some suggestions for using them in your day-to-day life, and information on how to learn more about them. Be sure to use your journal or the journal pages in this book to write down any notes, thoughts, and feelings as you move through this section.*

1) Take Responsibility

The most important thing to recognize before making any critical changes in your life is that YOU are responsible for your life. No one can take that from you (and you cannot take that from anyone). Reading this book, and any previous personal growth work you have done throughout your life are true signs you are on a path of claiming responsibility for your life. *Claiming personal responsibility is a critical step in your personal evolution.*

You are here because you have made choices that have led you here. You are the only person who can make choices for you, and you came here for a purpose, with purpose, and on purpose. Everything you have done up to this point (and will continue to do throughout your personal journey) is up to you, and it all supports your life's purpose!

You are not a victim of circumstances, life, other people, places or things; and you are *just* as important as the Queen of England, Oprah Winfrey, His Holiness the Dalai Lama, every tree, animal, drop of water, blade of grass, star system, and planetary body in the Universe.

Furthermore, if *you* are responsible for *your* choices in your life, then nothing can actually be done "to you." Life can only happen *for* you. Everything that happens in your life can only happen to support *your* choices. On some level, you have created everything you have ever experienced, will ever experience, and are experiencing right now.

You must take responsibility to evolve. If this is difficult for you to grasp at this point, sit with this idea, breathe into your heart (see the Heart-Centered Breathing exercise on p. 30), and journal about your thoughts surrounding it.

Do your best to allow this idea to sink in… Nobody else can live your life for you. You can choose to be your own best friend or worst enemy. It actually is a choice. Whatever *you* do, create, choose, act upon, or accept in *your* life is *your* responsibility. Take a deep breath and choose wisely.

2) <u>Heart-Centered Breathing</u>

This is one of my all-time favorite breathing exercises. I have used many different centering tools over the years, and so far none compares to how much I gain from this exercise.

Heart-Centered Breathing Exercise:

> 1) Take a few deep breaths. As you breathe in and out, visualize the space around your heart and breathe into it.
>
> 2) As you breathe in and out from your heart, think about something or someone you appreciate deeply and are grateful for. Breathe the gratitude you are feeling into and out of your heart.
>
> 3) Lock in the new feeling as you continue to breathe the gratitude in and out through your heart. As you continue this breathing, notice as you relax and become more in-tune with your heart.

The above exercise was adapted from *heartmath.org*, a non-profit organization that studies and teaches ways to bring your heart into a coherent place of deep, supportive relaxation to handle and/or prevent stress, anxiety, depression, and more. Check out the organization for more information, books, CDs, and other Heart Math tools to support you.

3) <u>Journaling</u>

To journal is to write down your deepest thoughts and feelings as if you are the only person who will ever see what you are writing. To avoid journaling, some people are concerned someone else will read it. That thought could simply be fear talking, and may hold you back from looking deeply at your innermost thoughts and feelings. If this is a concern, use a locked diary, a hidden place to keep your journal, or a program on your computer that contains a password to get into it.

By writing things down, you can get to the core of your thoughts. If you don't write your thoughts down or talk about them, they can swirl around in your mind chaotically, or become forced into the back of your mind, where they may become dark secrets or unsupportive beliefs.

I call journaling "therapy without the therapist." Journaling can help you get things out in the open, can help move and motivate you into your higher purpose, or can help you "dialogue on paper" with people, financial situations, animals, or other situations in your life to work things out with them more clearly, gently, and easily.

Consider journaling every day for 10-20 minutes for 30 days (*The Artist's Way*, by Julia Cameron, is a great book to support this process). This daily journaling can help you create a habit of getting your thoughts on paper while supporting you through the initial discomfort of journaling. It can also get you to a place of listening more clearly and intentionally to your thoughts. When you first begin writing things down, you might find you feel silly or ridiculous. These thoughts are simply egoic fears trying to keep you from moving out of your comfort zone. Push beyond them; they are only at the surface of what you are trying to move into and through.

<u>*Getting Started*</u>

First, purchase a notebook, journal, or diary you can look forward to picking up every day. Choose one that creates comfort or joy when you see the cover. It could have your favorite color, animal, plant, tree, location, quote, or saying on the cover, or something that simply makes you smile. Just be sure you pick something you are excited about using.

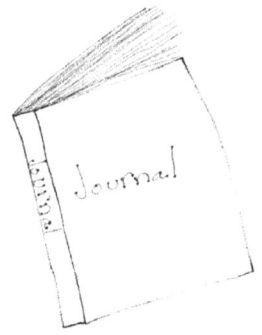

I have been journaling since early childhood and sometimes I buy the inexpensive "Composition Book" notebooks from the school section of the store, and other times, I buy a fancy journal at a bookstore. I love receiving journals as gifts and have often purchased them at garage sales. I know I will eventually use the journal, or I will gift it to someone else.

Next, spend some time with your journal just letting the idea of writing in it sink in. While you are contemplating writing in your journal, pick a time of day when you can have at least 10-20 minutes of free time. It could be first thing in the morning when you wake up, right before you go to bed at night, during your lunch break, whatever works for you. You might even set a clock or schedule it to remind you for the first few days or until it becomes a habit.

Begin writing your thoughts as they come to you. Do not try to edit them. Do not think too much about what you are writing. Do not even re-read your words. Just write your immediate thoughts to get into the habit of journaling. The purpose of journaling is not to judge, validate, or criticize yourself; it is simply one of the most effective ways to get things out of your head and into the circulation of release. Spend 10-20 minutes doing this every day for 30 days and notice how it can gently support you in releasing old patterns and belief structures.

Once you have done this for 30 days, consider writing more deeply personal things you are ready to release. Allow the deeper and more intimate thoughts to come out. Start spending more time in the process of releasing old patterns instead of writing random thoughts as they come to you.

Use journaling as a tool to support you in discovering your thoughts around issues that have held you back in the past. Use it as a tool to help you uncover deep-seated fears and other emotions. Allow it to support you in being your own "therapist" of sorts as you uncover any *pain-bodies* (Terms p. 137) that would otherwise hold you hostage in a pattern of stuck emotion or physical pain. Be sure to seek support from a professional if things become too uncomfortable to handle on your own. Also, be gentle with yourself as you work through your feelings and needs.

Journaling, like all other tools, can be used on its own or in conjunction with other tools to support your growth, transformation, and personal evolution.

4) Emotional Freedom Technique (EFT)

"*Emotional Freedom Technique*," (Terms p. 137) also known as "tapping," is a technique that was made popular and accessible to the public by Gary Craig. I have found this mode of support to be very powerful; often I have found things shift within one session of using this tool.

The general idea is to tap on certain acupuncture points while stating something that you are ready to move through. Since becoming certified in this technique, I have noticed that the way in which I move through things has become more gentle and immediate. It took me a few months to become regular about using it, but once I did, I discovered it could be used for anything.

You can find all kinds of information and guidance online, in books, and through courses. Online, go to YouTube, type "EFT" or "Emotional Freedom Technique" in the search, and explore some of the many videos available. Also, check out *eftuniverse.com*. If you prefer books, go to any library or book store to find information about this technique.

I use this tool on a regular basis. Once you are comfortable using it, you can even tap as a surrogate for those who are not able to tap for themselves, such as babies, children, and the elderly or disabled.

5) The Corral Exercise

This concept came to me one day to get clear of the "yamma-yamma" of my mind, to "get out of my own 'why'", and to accept that I am *more than* my body and mind.

The best way to describe it is to simply guide you through it. You may want to be alone or with someone you completely trust while going through this exercise. Avoid going through it with anyone with whom you may have major issues or discomfort. *Be sure you have at least an hour free of distractions to go through it.* Also, I suggest you simply do the exercise *as* you are reading it, instead of reading ahead.

The Corral Exercise:

To prepare:
A) Gather two clean, blank (unlined) sheets of paper and a writing instrument and have a flat surface available for writing.

B) Sit in a comfortable position and do "Heart-Centered Breathing" (as described on p. 30).

C) Now, think about only ONE issue you have felt trapped by or stuck in. *You can do this exercise with any or all issues, but I recommend focusing on one at a time.*

D) Once you have the one issue clear in your mind, set one of the sheets of paper aside.

E) On the first sheet, draw a large oval (your "corral") with some space around the outside of it.

Then:
1) Inside the corral draw a small figure in the center representing you.

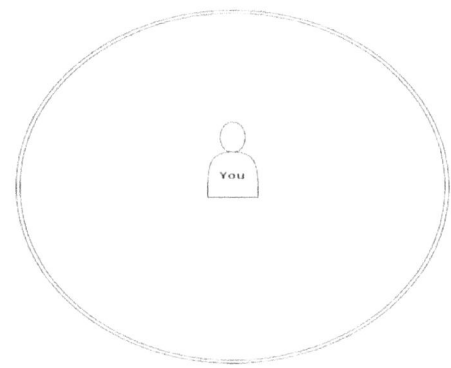

2) Anywhere on the page, write one sentence or word that describes the "issue."

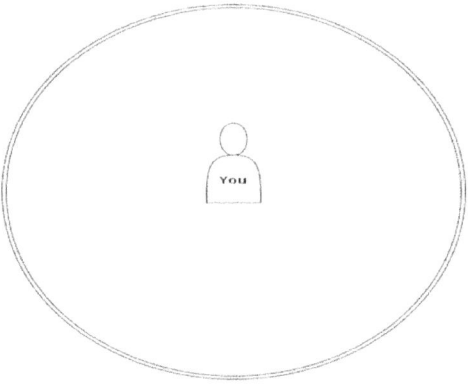

The Issue

3) Just <u>outside</u> the corral, draw small figures or "heads" to represent all the negative voices and thoughts you hear in your head about this issue.

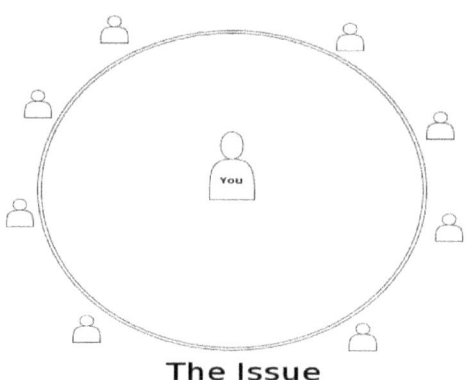

The Issue

NOTE: *As you draw each head/figure, you can say things out loud like:*

"This thought started when I was _____."

"This idea was created when _____ happened."

"I started believing this because of what _____ told me when I was little."

"This issue seems to be perpetuated by _____."

And so on.

---

4) You can even name the figures that represent the thoughts that come up around the issue. Write "my boss"; "my mom/dad"; "my partner"; "my child"; "my siblings"; etc, above or around the figures.

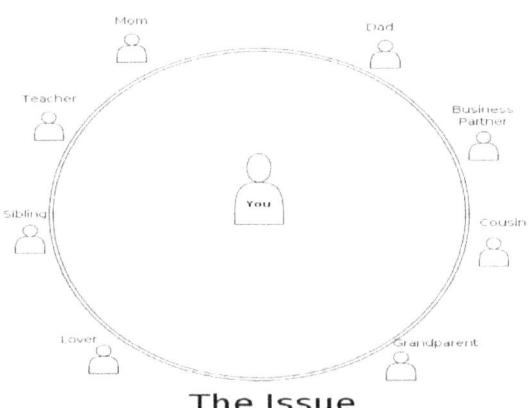

The Issue

Take your time with this process. The issue has built up over time; it could take a little while to get through all the thoughts you have about it and get them onto the paper.

> **NOTE:** *And remember, this is YOUR process, no one else's. You do not have to share this with anyone. If you wish, you can burn, tear up, or throw away the paper once the exercise is over.*

5) Now, <u>inside</u> the corral and all around "yourself," write the word "why?" as many times as you feel like writing it. As you write this word, begin listening to your thoughts around this particular issue.

The Issue

> **NOTE:** *The reason for the word "why" is to remind you that "why" is the most hopeless question in our language. It keeps us trapped. Have you ever tried to answer a three-year-old every time they ask "why"? It becomes a battle of wits and will. It is a never-ending question that cannot be answered. And yet, we often find ourselves trapped in the question, "why?" and keep ourselves stuck trying to answer it!*

How does it make you feel when you try to get out of this mode of thinking? (*Note your thoughts in the margins of the drawing you are working on.*)

6) Write some of your thoughts and feelings around "yourself" inside the corral. (*It does not matter if the words overlap or become unintelligible – just get them out of your head and onto the paper.*)

Things like, "I'm not good enough (smart enough, strong enough, small enough, big enough, etc.) to get through this." Or, "Why me?" "I hate my job," "I can't stand the way I look," "Prove it!" "When will you change?" And so on. Even add more "Whys" if you feel like it.

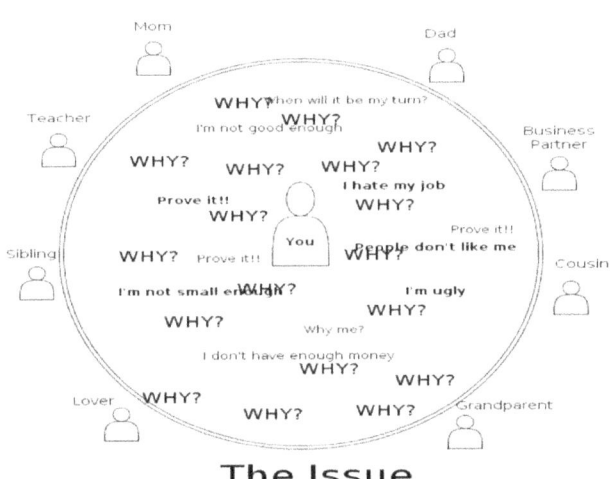

The Issue

Begin to notice when a thought or phrase brings about some deeper insight to the issue. Breathe into the thought and just open yourself to any awareness that decides to show up. You can even write those thoughts inside the circle.

IMPORTANT NOTE: DON'T QUIT NOW!! KEEP GOING!! *You may feel like running away, or something might be happening to stop your process, but now is the most crucial moment in this exercise. This trapped feeling is the reason you are doing this exercise.*

The moment you start to feel nervous, anxious, or like you want to get away is when something is about to shift! **Keep moving forward!**

7) Be open to what you are feeling. Write the feelings down on the outside of the corral. Are you feeling scared, uncomfortable, angry, sad, frustrated, bored, stupid, anxious, or hopeless? Write it down.

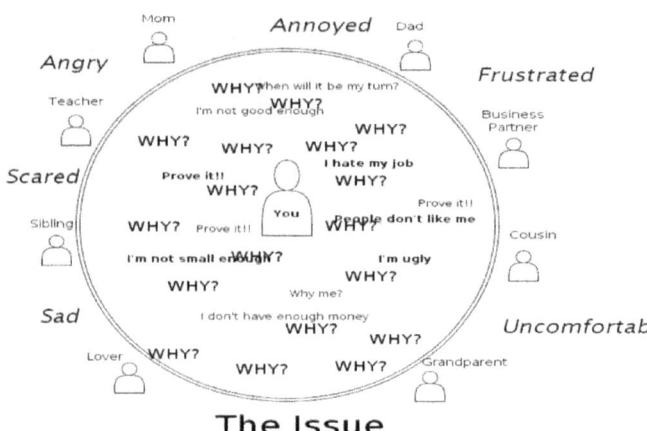

Be with it. Breathe through it. Allow the thoughts to move through you. These are the deepest, egoic thoughts that are holding you trapped inside this issue. Be present. Allow. Breathe. Stretch. Drink some water. Come right back to the exercise and write whatever you have left around this issue.

8) You may even notice some words like "curious," "excited," and "hopeful" show up in your thoughts. Write those down too.

After you feel like you have written all you can about the thoughts in your head around this subject, look at the paper. NO WONDER you have been stuck! That jumbled-up mass of words and faces represents your mind dealing with just one issue!

Now, set the first sheet of paper to the side and take out the other sheet of paper. Notice the blank, clean, clear space.

In the center of the page, draw a figure representing "My Whole, Complete, Perfect, Beautiful Self" with nothing else around it.

Would you like to feel that open and clear around this thought/belief/issue that has held you trapped? If the answer is yes, set aside both sheets of paper and take a very deep breath. Sit comfortably with this book in your hands. Breathe again deeply. Read the following meditation and then do the meditation on your own, or have someone else read it for you.

NOTE: To listen to me leading the following meditation, please go to *terrabundance.com*, go to the meditation page, and find a link for 'The Corral Meditation'.

The Corral Meditation:

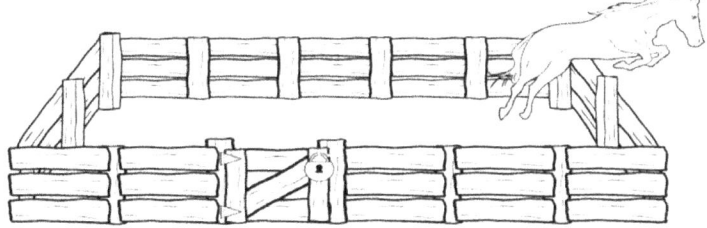

Close your eyes and visualize yourself standing in the center of a corral. Think about the issue you just moved through in the Corral Exercise. As you see yourself there, notice the image of another person about 100 feet from you, standing outside the corral. This other person is shining with a beautiful light that seems to be coming from nowhere and everywhere. You cannot quite see the person, but it seems like a familiar energy. Start to walk toward the bright, shining person.

Suddenly, you notice the sounds of people shouting at you the reasons you cannot leave the "safety" of your corral. They yell mean and aggressive, judgmental things to you. "You are silly to try to move through this." "You don't deserve to let go of this thought!" "Are you crazy?" "You can never get out of this corral!" "You're not good enough!" And so on... (all of the negative thoughts you wrote down on your paper earlier).

Then, notice the person outside the corral beckoning you to come out and play. You are drawn to the other person. You want to be free like that person. You find that the other voices are being drowned out by a soft, melodic sound that also seems to be coming from everywhere and nowhere.

Suddenly, you realize the other person is YOU! It is your Future Self, only moments from now. You are free and happy. You want to reach that Future Self!

Your Future Self holds the awareness for you that you have already escaped from the trap of the corral that holds you captive. Your Future Self beckons you.

Now, decide how you will get out of the corral. Will you run hard and fast through the people and the fence? Will you leap high in the air and over them? Will you push your way through until you are out?

Will you silence the voices until there are none? Will you open your heart and let your love shine out to all of the voices? Will you teleport from the corral to the outside? Will you build a bridge to climb out? What is your safest way to reach the future you? There is no wrong way to do it. Just DO it. NOW.

When you find yourself standing in front of your shining Future Self, allow it to gently embrace you. Your Future Self whispers in your ear, "I knew you would make it! Congratulations." Find yourself melting into your Future Self, and your Future Self melting into you. You are now that Self.

Look behind you and see the corral… It is just a tiny speck, a reminder of what you have accomplished. You are free from those voices. Now, whenever you feel those old voices and thoughts come back, remember, you are no longer trapped by them. You know you can move past them. You can thank the voices and old patterns and then walk away, leap out, levitate over, teleport out again, just like the first time. You've done it once, so you know you can do it again!

Know you are safe and clear of those beliefs that once held you trapped. You have changed your past by stepping into your new Future Self. You are FREE!

Breathe deeply. At this time, remember that you are fragile, like a newborn baby. As you move through the next few days, be as kind and gentle to yourself as you would be to that newborn baby. Set clear boundaries and allow yourself to move beyond the old patterns and voices that have held you back at other times. Just keep remembering this meditation and create a mantra that supports the new place you are carving out for yourself.

One of my favorite mantras is, "I am Life's Purpose, I am Life, I am!" I repeat it over and over when I need to remember my Divinity. We are all Life's Purpose!

6) <u>Cleansing/Clearing Bath or Shower</u>

Baths and showers can help clean off old energy as well as clean your body. When you bathe or shower, imagine all of the old stuff, beliefs, patterns, issues, pain-bodies, etc. coming out of your skin, your body, and your energy field and flowing into the water and down the drain.

- o Bath salts, bath beads, bath fizzies, bubble bath, incense, peaceful music, and more can be used to support a relaxing, comfortable atmosphere.
- o If you like scents when you bathe, I suggest you find the highest quality, therapeutic, food grade essential oils (TFGEO) to use. You can safely use many TFGEO on your body, in your food and water, in smoothies, and more. I personally recommend and use Young Living Oils and DoTerra Oils. (Be sure you know which ones are safe for you to use. Some people react adversely to some oils. Test them on a small patch of skin before using it in your food or your bath.)
- o You can find a really great color bath product at: *colourenergy.com/bath_products.html*. (Do not use food coloring as it will stain your body and tub.)
- o You can also surround your tub with crystals and other energetic tools such as small statues, shells, candles, incense, etc., to support the kind of energy you are choosing to create.

7) Meditation

Some popular types of meditation include: yoga nidra, transcendental (TM), mindfulness, heart-centered, religious, trance, tantric, inclusive, dualistic, awakening, and many more.

Some traditions that study and practice meditation include: Buddhism, Baha'i, Yoga, Tantra, Christianity, Hinduism, New Thought, Islam, Jainism, Judaism, New Age, Sikhism, Taoism, and more.

Definition of Meditation/Meditate-

"1) to engage in contemplation or reflection

2) to engage in mental exercise (as concentration on one's breathing or repetition of a mantra) for the purpose of reaching a heightened level of spiritual awareness" (The Miriam-Webster Dictionary).

There are nearly unlimited meditation tips, tools, CDs, books, and classes to choose from. If you are interested in learning more about this tool, I suggest you talk to someone who has been trained in or has practiced meditation, and/or find a class, CD, DVD, or YouTube video, to support you.

NOTE: *This may go without saying, but I will say it anyway: Do not practice any form of meditation while driving or doing anything else requiring your full attention.*

"*To meditate does not mean to fight with a problem. To meditate means to observe. Your smile proves it. It proves that you are being gentle with yourself, that the sun of awareness is shining in you, that you have control of your situation.*

You are yourself, and you have acquired some peace."

~Thich Nhat Hanh

8) Yoga

The *Miriam-Webster Dictionary* defines Yoga as:

"*1. a school of Hindu philosophy advocating and prescribing a course of physical and mental disciplines for attaining liberation from the material world and union of the self with the Supreme Being or ultimate principle.*

2. any of the methods or disciplines prescribed, especially a series of postures and breathing exercises practiced to achieve control of the body and mind, tranquillity, etc.

3. union of the self with the Supreme Being or ultimate principle."

Some popular types of yoga include: Iyengar yoga, Yoga Nidra, Bikram/hot yoga, ashtanga yoga, jivamukti yoga, kundalini yoga, laughter yoga, tantra yoga, power yoga, and many more.

There is so much information available about yoga. There are tips, tools, CDs, books, classes, and more to choose from. Here are a few websites to check out:

- *yogajournal.com*
- *yogaalliance.org*
- *livewithyoga.net*
- *americanyogaassociation.org*

I also suggest you talk to someone who has been trained in or practiced yoga, or find a class, CD, video, or other tool to support you in learning more about it. Check online for local yoga instructors and classes. If you are not able to go online, check with a local fitness spa, community center, health food store, or library. You can also check bulletin boards at local coffee shops, bookstores, New Thought churches, spiritual organizations, and Yoga centers. Many places will post information about classes, books, DVDs, YouTube videos, and local instructors, as well as sources for yoga props such as yoga mats, blocks for support, straps, etc.

9) Support Groups and Individuals

The following are just a few of the many different types of therapy and support available:

Teachers, mentors, parents, friends, life coaches, Religious Science Practitioners, counselors, therapists, 12-step programs, support groups for a particular issue, acupuncture, massage, chiropractic, Reiki and other bodywork, energy healers/revealers, and so much more.

I suggest you research and try out various kinds of therapy, support groups, and relaxation or bodywork to discover what might be best for you. Try each at least a few times before you decide to discontinue it (unless, of course, you just really feel averse to it right away).

10) <u>Your Intention for Food, Water & Other Life-Energy</u>

You may be aware that most people consider water to be essential to our well-being, along with healthy eating and rest. Yet, do you know how much water is enough for *you*? What does "healthy eating" actually mean for *you*? How *much* rest? Obviously those ideas can vary from person to person, and situation to situation. Every human has a personal way of looking at life, and each person has a personal relationship to food, eating habits, health, etc.

This is how I choose to look at it: *The Law of Attraction* (Terms p. 137) simply states, "Thoughts are things." In other words, whatever thoughts are held in your mind will show up in your life. Your intentions (your repetitive, ongoing thoughts) are how you create your experiences in your life. If you decide something is "good" or "bad" for you, it will be, no matter how much proof or denial you hear from others. It is only true because you believe it is true. How you eat, drink, rest, and experience your life essentially comes down to your thoughts and intentions.

Henry Ford is attributed with saying, "If you think you can do a thing, or think you can't do a thing, you're right!" And Dr. Wayne Dyer has been quoted as saying, "Our intention creates our reality." Whatever *you* think works or does not work for *you* is correct for *you*.

I have read about a healthy, happy man who gets everything he needs from the energy of the sun and does not eat or drink anything. I have heard about "breatharians" who live entirely from the breath they take in and out. I personally know many raw foodists, vegetarians, and vegans, as well as people who eat pretty much anything they desire, who all lead happy, healthy lives and would swear their way is the only way to live. *And every one of them is correct!* Their way is the only way for *them* to live. If you choose to believe in any one of those ways, in several of them, or even make one up for yourself, you will be correct, so long as you fully *believe* in your choice.

Simply decide what works for you and live by it. If you decide to change it, then change it. You are the creator of your life and the one who gets to live it. Live it according to where your heart guides you, where your instinct steers you, where you feel called from deep within you, without judgment or the need to prove your point to anyone else.

Remember that you are responsible for your choices, so I suggest that you really look deeply into your heart to know what is "right" for you.

One more suggestion: Try blessing whatever you enjoy eating or drinking with the Life-Source Energy that supports your best and highest experience of life. Hold your hands out over your food and drink, take a deep breath in and out through your heart, talk to what you are about to ingest and communicate that your substance and its substance are going to work together to live out your purpose. Thank the food (water, etc.), accept the gift it is giving you, and enjoy every single mouthful as a life-giving, life-supporting, beautiful, wonderful blessing. My prayer before ingesting anything into my body is, "I now bless this food (water, etc.) for the nourishment of my body. Thank you to those who gave their lives so that I may eat and thrive. Thank you for the life-supporting, life-enriching energy in this food (or drink). I take it in and I live out my purpose, fully supported on all levels. And so it is."

11) <u>Acceptance</u>

"I accept, I allow, I embrace..."

Decide now that you are willing to be supported by your guides, by the God of your understanding, by yourself, by your friends, by your angels, by beings seen and unseen who enter your field to provide loving, nurturing support and guidance.

In my opinion, this is the second most important thing you can do to become empowered in any stage of your life; the most important being "taking responsibility." When you feel stuck, open your heart to what is being provided to support you. LOOK for the support and ACCEPT it when it shows up. TRUST that it will always show up. You have made it this far somehow. Decide now to recognize that one of the possible reasons is because you are here for a purpose. *Follow* your heart, *listen* to your inner wisdom, and *allow* yourself to be supported.

12) Gratitude!

My family practices getting together on Tuesday mornings to give thanks for our lives and speak out loud anything specific that we are grateful for. We call the day "Grati-Tuesday" and we all do our best to be present for it every week, even if some of us are not home, are sleepy, are wide awake, are annoyed with each other, are happy, are feeling sad, or are excited to be together.

We start with a small chime being rung by the first person who makes it to the living room. We all sit down and say good morning to each other. We read the "10 things you can do to contribute to Peace" from Marshall Rosenberg's book, *Nonviolent Communication*. We each speak out loud our gratitudes. We each speak an affirmation for the day. We take a moment of silence. We sing three ohms and end with Namaste.

This practice has changed each one of our lives in some way, from the 5-year-old (who has an almost Pavlovian response to the chime we ring in the mornings. If we ring it any other time during the day, he jokingly sits down and starts naming things he is grateful for) to each of the teens and adults.

I suggest you find some time each week (or each day), with or without family, to practice being grateful for the many things in your life that support you and keep you balanced and whole. You may find your list getting longer every time you do it; and gratitude will eventually be what you turn to during crucial moments in your life. Also, if you write down your gratitudes daily for a week, month, or year, you will likely be astounded at the number and variety of things you are grateful for. Gratitude is one of my favorite weekly family practices, and I personally enjoy doing my gratitudes EVERY day.

13) <u>Create Your Own Toolbox</u>

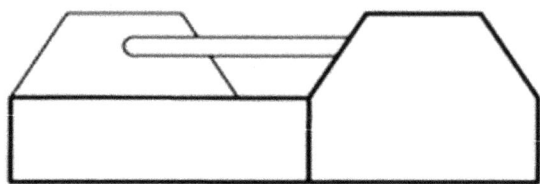

Some suggestions for creating your own toolbox:
- o   Create your own tools for each stage, starting on p. 139.
- o   Add tools that you have heard about throughout your life.
- o   Write notes about your favorite tools in a separate journal.
- o   Send any tools you would like to share with others to me at *terrabundance.com*. With your permission, I may cite you in future "Butterfly Toolbox" books and/or on my website.

Egg Stage Conclusion:

The most important goal in the Egg Stage is to move beyond your comfort zones and figure out what truly works for *you*. The takeaways from this stage are: **embrace the idea of change as a constant, and nurture yourself.**

In this stage, you have learned to practice patience, to embrace the idea of allowing change, and to support yourself the way you would if you were a baby or young toddler.

Just think if you saw a baby crying for help, you would not just walk by. You would offer it support. You also would not laugh at, push, or punish a baby if they did not learn to crawl or walk the first time they tried. This stage reminds you to give yourself the same love, support, patience, and kindness you would give to a baby learning to crawl, walk, or talk.

Now, it is time to be sure you are sufficiently complete with the Egg Stage. If you feel the need to stay with this stage for now, consider going through some of the exercises again and see if you notice something you may have missed before. Or, try doing some of the exercises in a different way. Before moving into the Caterpillar Stage, check in with yourself. Are you feeling fragile, weak, tired, scared, shaky, nervous, or overwhelmed? Do you feel like you have fully moved through the Egg Stage? Do you feel supported?

The next stage requires energy and a willingness to step even more fully out of your comfort zone. You will want to start the next stage in an empowered and grounded space. You want to feel (at least a little bit) excited, motivated, and ready to move on.

Take your time, be patient, enjoy the journey, and be at peace with yourself. And only *then* move on to the next stage.

JOURNAL SECTION-
Egg Stage

II. Caterpillar Stage

*"The caterpillar does all the work,
but the butterfly gets all the publicity."
~George Carlin*

In the Caterpillar Stage of your personal journey, you feel hungry for all things new to read or listen to. You may seek out people to talk to about the new things you are discovering, or you simply love trying new things. You cannot seem to get enough, and you strive for more awareness.

Caterpillar Stage Main Focus:
Transformation and Paying Attention

In the Caterpillar Stage, you might feel hungry for information, excited to try something new, and even a little nervous. You might not know where to go or whom to trust, but you still look forward to taking the steps to learn more about the new possibilities available in your life.

The Caterpillar Stage is where you might re-discover the child inside who loves to **learn and try new things**. It's a great place to become excited again about meeting new people and going places you have never been before. You might even remember things you wanted to do when you were younger, but never felt supported or ready to try them. Now is the time! You are in a stage where trying new things is essentially important and necessary for your personal growth.

Take those art or music lessons you were always afraid to take. Try that pottery or yoga class. Go back to school and get your degree. Start talking to people who are doing the things you always wanted to do. Get a job working in a place that feeds your deepest soul desires.

It may seem a little daring or out of your comfort zone, yet, remember you have just gotten through the Egg Stage! You can do so much more than you ever thought you could before! Just give it a chance. If you find yourself at a seeming dead end, do not give up. Yoda says, "Try not. Do, or do not. There is no try." And Thomas Edison said about inventing the light bulb, "I didn't fail 1,000 times. The light bulb was an invention with 1,000 steps." Dream big! The possibilities are endless!

Chakras for the Caterpillar Stage

In this stage, you are working with chakras 4, 4½, and 5. (Heart/Green, High-Heart/Turquoise or Pink, and Throat/Light or Bright Blue) These are the three chakras that define how you perform and show up in the outside world. They help create and form your passion and purpose, and support you in communicating them out from your energy field and into the world.

You develop and strengthen the 4th through 5th chakras based on how you live from the first three chakras. Once you have shifted your perspectives and patterns in the first three chakras, it is simply a part of the continuation process to shift in the following chakras.

Caterpillar Stage Check-In:
Am I Willing?

One way to decide if you are ready for this stage is to sit quietly and breathe. Check in with your inner guidance and tune into your thoughts, your feelings, and your physical body. Write any answers or feelings you may have about the below questions in your personal journal, the journal at the end of this chapter (p. 79), or in the main journal in back of this book (pp. 143-164). Ask yourself:

1) Do I feel hungry for any and all information I can find about something new I am interested in or just learned about?

2) Have I recently come out of an old pattern and want to try a new way of looking at and experiencing my life?

3) Am I excited (and maybe a little nervous) about any synchronicities that have been happening lately?

4) Have I noticed any changes in the people I choose to surround myself with?

5) Do I feel like I have so much to learn, yet still look forward to the growth?

6) Am I willing to talk with and learn from others who seem to have what I desire?

7) Am I willing to step out of my comfort zones and allow myself to be guided?

If you answered "yes" to at least two of the above questions, you are most likely in the Caterpillar Stage. As you move through this stage, you may find each one of those questions coming up again. When you are willing to say "yes" to them, you are steadily stepping into a new way of creating and seeing your life.

Congratulations! You have made it through the Egg Stage and you are now stepping onto the path of the Caterpillar!

Embrace the Caterpillar Stage:

Once you have decided you are ready to move into the Caterpillar Stage, it is time to **remain open to change**. In the Egg Stage, you made a choice to make a change, and now is the time to accept the changes as they happen. And they can happen slowly or quickly.

There is no "right" or "wrong" way to move through this (or any other) stage. **Take as much time as you need**, and really allow yourself to absorb as much as you can through this stage -- ALL of the stages for that matter!

Caterpillars steadily take in as much food (information in your case) as they need before it is time to move into the cocoon. Be willing to do the same for yourself. Steadily take in as much information as you can, and be very aware and open to anything that might "feed you" as you move through the Caterpillar Stage.

Affirmation for the Caterpillar Stage:

Breathe in and out from your heart and say to yourself out loud:

"I am open to a new adventure to feed my body, mind, and spirit. I am willing to embrace new information as it enters gently into my personal awareness. I am willing to carefully ingest, digest, and absorb the information coming to me through this process. I welcome new experiences, awarenesses, and ideas that show up as I open to new possibilities for my life."

Tools for the Caterpillar Stage:

- *Notes for this stage can be made on pp. 79-83.*
- *You can add your own tools for this stage on p. 140.*
- *Draw "tools" to go into your toolbox below.*
- *Creative Suggestion: To create a sacred, personal space, build an altar with some of your favorite stones and/or personal items. Search online for some ideas.*

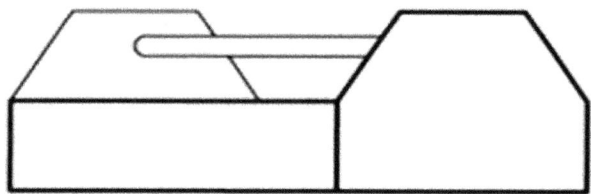

1) High-Heart Chakra/Assemblage Point (p. 63)
2) Inspiration (p. 66)
3) Trying Something New (p. 69)
4) Challenging Yourself (p. 70)
5) The Enneagram (p. 71)
6) Synchronicities ("Coincidences") (p. 72)
7) Gratitude and Planting Seeds (p. 77)

Below are descriptions of The Caterpillar Stage Tools, *some suggestions for using them in your day-to-day life, and information on how to learn more about them. Be sure to use your journal or the journal pages in this book to write down any notes, thoughts, and feelings as you move through this Stage.*

1) High-Heart Chakra/Assemblage Point

Carlos Castaneda is the first person I know of who talked about the Assemblage Point. Much study and scientific data has been discovered about it over the years, and I have my own theories about it as well.

From *theassemblagepoint.com*: *"...as a compound system, the human body emits a great variety of frequencies. All synchronized vibrating systems have an epicenter... In us, this epicenter is called the Human Assemblage Point. It is concentrated at the center of the chest for the optimum physical and psychological health of human beings. The shape and power of the human energy field is inseparably connected with this place. Through the Assemblage Point there passes a compacted bundle of energy threads or strings. These fan out and connect to our environment. They serve the role of our perceptual energy, connecting us to our surrounding environment, such as: people, objects, and other energies."*

According to scholars, authors, and others who discuss the Assemblage Point, it is located somewhere between the heart center/chakra and the throat center/chakra (*see image on p.64*). I (and many others) call that point the "high-heart" chakra. It is the "seat of truth" in the body, where the passion and desire of the heart chakra is bridged to be communicated through the throat chakra and out into the world.

Assemblage Point Exercise:

Take a moment to touch that place above your heart. It is also known as the thymus center which, when firmly tapped on, can activate your immune system. Go ahead and tap on it to tune in to that space, to activate your immune system, and to create a connection to your Personal Assemblage Point.

If you are not sure exactly where it is, simply tap in that general area. You may notice a sensation of opening or awakening something there.

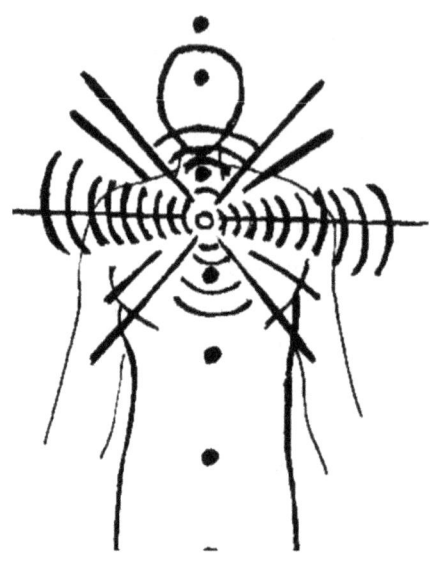

Now, as you are tapping that area, think about your own personal place of power, the place of highest awareness in your life, your biggest strength or calling.

Put your hand or hands on your high heart area, breathe deeply and ask yourself: What do I feel I am meant to share with the world? What fills my heart and body with deep joy when I think about it? Is it to sing and open hearts? Is it to speak to the masses about something? Is it to paint, draw or create beautiful art that connects people? Is it to raise amazing children to live out their passion and purpose? Is it to be a firefighter or doctor, an astronaut or a lawyer? Is it to network with others, or to travel the world? Is it to create amazing food to support people to thrive and become their best and highest calling? Is it to teach something brand new to the world? Is it to challenge people to step into their own highest place of love and support, passion and purpose? Or is it simply—and profoundly—to smile with love on all whom I meet?

Pay attention to the things you *love* to do more than *anything* else. If you did not have to think about finances, what would you be doing with your life? What would you do if you knew you could not fail? Write down your thoughts and answers. *That* is the energy that shines forth from your Assemblage Point to support you in living out your purpose and passion. That alignment is known as your Personal Point of Power.

Now that you have an idea of your highest place of passion and purpose, breathe deeply into your high-heart area while continuing to touch that place with the palm of your hand (or hands). Take another deep breath while thinking about your purpose and passion (your Personal Point of Power). Take one more deep breath while tuning in to your field (the area around you). Your physical and energetic Assemblage Point is now vibrating at its highest level and will begin calling all energies that vibrate at a similar rate (or have a similar calling) into your personal energy field. Those new vibrations will support you in releasing thoughts and beliefs from the past that might have held you back from living fully in your passion and purpose. Those vibrations will also support you in opening to all that you need to live and thrive in every area of your life. Take a deep breath and be grateful for your connection.

If you ever feel "out of sorts" or "off-kilter," it could be you have not tuned in with your Personal Point of Power in a while. Take a moment to do the above exercise again. Notice whether your focus has shifted (which will surely happen from time to time). Establish your connection and become re-aligned in your Personal Point of Power. If you can make it a regular practice to tune in to your high-heart chakra, I believe you can become much more solidly present in your daily life, and thrive more consistently in your passion and purpose.

Please take a few moments to *center and ground yourself* in this new energy/awareness before moving on to the next tools.

2) Inspiration

There are so many sources of inspiration available when we take the time to notice the world around us. Some inspirations might include your favorite books, songs, quotes, classes, teachers, spiritual leaders, or other people doing something you might be considering doing in your own life. Here are a few of my favorite inspirational tools:

- *Books*

Books are such a great source of inspiration. Below is a list of my top 10 favorite inspirational books (not in any particular order). I have read many of them more than once, and I have received something new from them each time. These are not, of course, the only books I recommend reading, but this is a really good place to start. You can find them new at bookstores, New Thought centers and churches, and online, or used at thrift stores, used book stores, or on *amazon.com*.

- *Jonathan Livingston Seagull,* Richard Bach
- *Illusions,* Richard Bach
- *The Four Agreements,* Don Miguel Ruiz
- *A New Earth,* Eckhart Tolle
- *The Celestine Prophecy,* James Redfield
- *The Voice of Knowledge,* Don Miguel Ruiz
- *Nonviolent Communication,* Marshall Rosenberg
- *This Thing Called You,* Ernest Holmes
- *Codependent No More,* Melody Beattie
- *Animal Speak,* Ted Andrews

- *Music*

As a life-long musician, writing and listening to music is where I gain some of my deepest inspiration. The following musicians are not the only musicians I listen to, but they are the ones I tend to turn to first. You can find their music in stores, New Thought communities, online at their personal websites, through *amazon.com*, iTunes and – for a quick fix – on YouTube, Google Play, Pandora, UnityFM, GrooveShark, Spotify, or other music streaming sites.

In no particular order:

Michael Franti, John Lennon, Jana Stanfield, Faith Rivera, Rickie Byars Beckwith, Brett Mikels, Ash Ruiz, Here II Here, Almine, Ray LaMontagne, Robert Gass, any Shapeshifter/Visionary Music CDs, Stephen Halpern, Karen Drucker, Devotion, David Roth, David Ault, Michael Stillwater, Mahalia Jackson, Deuter, Etta James, Eva Cassidy, Jan Garrett and JD Martin, The Max Ribner Band, k.d. lang, Jami Lula, Jenny Bird, Michael Mandrell, Elijah Ray, any Kirtan music, Gypsy Soul, 4 Stories High, Laura Berman, Craig Benelli, Talib Kweli, Daniel Nahmod, Aretha Franklin, Tom Kenyon, Enigma, Jonathan Goldman, Laura Ivancie, Nathen Aswell, Kelly Corsino, Luminaries, Nahko and Medicine for the People, Charles Sorgie, Amy Steinberg, **and so many more!**

For more information on some of the musicians listed above; plus many other great, conscious, inspirational/motivational musicians and groups, check out these websites:

- ➢ *Luminaryvoices.com*
- ➢ *Positivemusicassociation.com*
- ➢ *Empowerma.com*

- *Quotes and Stories*

Great quotes and stories about people who have been challenged- and then moved through those challenges to evolve and share their gifts with the world- are everywhere. I tend to find most of my inspirational favorites in books and on websites. I also receive daily inspirational quotes online. Below are the ones I appreciate the most:

* Websites and daily emails/insights:

➢ *Des.emory.edu/mfp/efficacynotgiveup.html*

➢ *Inspirationpeak.com*

➢ TUT's Notes from the Universe / *tut.com*

➢ Neale Donald Walsch / *nealedonaldwalsch.com*

➢ Motivation in a Minute / *motivationinaminute.com*

➢ Lissa Coffey / *coffeytalk.com*

➢ Abraham-Hicks Quotes / *abraham-hicks.com*

➢ Susan Buckley / *voiceofenthusiasm.com*

➢ The Hendricks Institute / *thehendricksinstitute.com*

- *Inspirational Movies*

A few of my favorite spiritual, interview-style, "learning" movies include:

➢ *What the Bleep Do We Know?*

➢ *The Secret*

➢ *Guru*

➢ *Living Luminaries*

➢ *One*

➢ *You Can Heal Your Life*

➢ *I Am.*

And for inspirational moviemakers, producers, actors, movies, and performers, check out these websites:

➢ *Gatecommunity.org*

➢ *Spiritualcinemacircle.com*

- *Inspirational Speakers and Authors*

Below are just a few of *many* motivational and inspirational speakers, authors and spiritual leaders who have inspired me and countless others.

Again, in no particular order:

Marianne Williamson, Eckhart Tolle, Jesus, Michael Beckwith, Neale Donald Walsch, Ram Dass, Rev. David Alexander, Martin Luther King, Jr., Muhammad, Lao Tzu, Almine, Masuru Emoto, David Ault, Buddha, Edwene Gaines, Gay Hendricks, Patch Adams, Oprah Winfrey, Louise L. Hay, Gandhi, Jim Carrey, Earnest Holmes, Don Miguel Ruiz, Earl Nightingale, Barbara Marx Hubbard, Jean Houston, Karen Drucker, Brene Brown, Gregg Braden, Byron Katie, Dan Millman, Deepak Chopra, Zig Ziglar, Wayne Dyer, His Holiness, The Dalai Lama…

For information on those and other inspirational speakers, check out:

- *Luminaryvoices.com*
- *Gatecommunity.org*
- *Ted.com*

You can also search online, or go to the library and ask for well-known motivational, inspirational, or spiritual speakers' books. Talks and presentations from inspirational and motivational speakers are also available on CD, DVD, YouTube, *amazon.com*, and their individual websites.

3) <u>Classes, Organizations, Groups</u>

Toastmasters, speech classes, acting classes, choirs, writing clubs, fitness clubs, neighborhood clubs, local outdoor/hiking/biking clubs, etc., are some of the types of groups you can get involved in to step outside of your comfort zone and meet others who are inspired by the same kinds of things you are inspired and motivated by. You can find them online by searching *meetup.com* or *craigslist.org* for your local area, or visit your local library bulletin boards, community centers, or through the Chamber of Commerce in your town.

To be daring, think of something you have never seen before, and start your own group or organization. List it on *meetup.com*, with your Chamber of Commerce, and your library. Put an ad in your local newspaper's classified section that says, "Searching for others who are interested in learning more about _____." Put an ad on *craigslist.org* (there is a listing for Craigslist in every major city in America), or list your interests on a *Facebook.com* profile, group, or page.

I met a woman who put an ad on Craigslist, "Looking for adult Indigos." I contacted her, and it turned out that I had *just* met her at a local house concert two days before I found the ad! The "coincidence" was too much to ignore. We were meant to know each other.

If you want to learn more about *anything*, start a study group, mastermind group, Meetup, or book club, and learn about it with others. By stepping out of your comfort zone, you could find exactly what you are looking for!

4) <u>Challenge Yourself!</u>

Try out for a play or a team sport, go to a local club and sing karaoke, join a Toastmasters group, sing in the shower or in the middle of the subway downtown. Do something outside your comfort zone just to prove to yourself you can get through it! Every time we challenge ourselves and get to the other side of something, we give ourselves a chance to learn more about how strong, powerful and courageous we are instead of focusing on how weak or shy we think we are. We are incredible, resilient, amazing beings, and we are capable of *so* much more than we generally give ourselves credit for!

Do something you have always wanted to do, but felt too scared to try. Do it for a week, once a week for a month, or every day for six months! Do the new thing several times before you decide whether or not it works for you. Take someone you trust along with you for the moral support if necessary. We can all "get by with a little help from our friends," say The Beatles. Why not? You will find you have much more to gain than to lose when you start expanding your personal borders.

5) The Enneagram

The enneagram (pronounced "ANY-a-gram") is a tool that has been a very useful for many people I know. The modern enneagram of 'personality type' is a development of modern psychology. It was created from a blend of many ancient spiritual and religious traditions, yet it doesn't claim to be a complete spiritual path. It does, however, focus on one element that is fundamental to all spiritual-emotional paths, seeking *self-knowledge* (which also *happens* to be the driving force in the Caterpillar Stage!)

According to many books about the enneagram, working with it involves presence, self-observation, and interpretation of your experiences within a larger, 'worldly' context. The enneagram names and describes in detail nine primary personality types and their interactions. Although there are differences and subtleties described by several authors, a common listing of the 9 personality types is as follows:

1 The Reformer

2 The Helper

3 The Achiever

4 The Individualist

5 The Investigator

6 The Loyalist

7 The Enthusiast

8 The Challenger

9 The Peacemaker

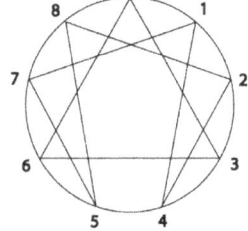

The enneagram can strengthen your confidence in your emotional and spiritual strong points, while at the same time, help raise questions about areas you might not want to accept at face value. A friend of mine is a strong Type 9 Peacemaker, and she was astounded to discover that she had, unknown to her, deep-seated anger that had shown up throughout her life as passive-aggressiveness. Addressing that "can of worms" has allowed her to create new choices in her interactions with people, and has made her a more compassionate and effective peacemaker.

If you'd like to pursue this for yourself, you could start by asking people you know if they work with the enneagram in their personal journey. You may be surprised how many say "yes" and then go on to talk about its usefulness!

Also, there are many great books on learning about and using the enneagram. Here are two I can recommend:

➢ *The Enneagram: Understanding Yourself and the Others in Your Life* by Helen Palmer

➢ *Personality Types: Using the Enneagram for Self Discovery* by Don Richard Riso & Russ Hudson.

There is also a free enneagram personality test available at: enneagraminstitute.com that can help get you started on identifying your type.

6) Synchronicity/"Coincidence"

"By seeing the beauty in every face, we lift others into their wisest self and increase the chances of hearing a synchronistic message."
~James Redfield

I often carry a journal with me, and throughout the day I write down all the events I usually would pass off as "just a coincidence." What I have found every time is that those "seeming coincidences" were the exact answers I had been asking or praying for! If I had not been paying close attention, they might have vanished or been overlooked.

We are magnets to our desires, "Law of Attraction Machines," and "Gurus of Creation!" We are capable of manifesting *anything* we put our goals, desires, energies, and focus on. We are always receiving guidance from *many* sources to make our dreams and goals a reality.

Pay attention! This book in your hands could be a "coincidence." The person sitting next to you could even be reading the same book! What if you noticed more synchronicities in your life? How do you think that might change your perspective on what you consider your reality?

Synchronicity can be one of the most delightful spiritual tools available to you, and all it takes to experience it is to pay attention! "Coincidences" generally lead us right where we need to go. *Pay attention to all of the synchronicities in your life. It opens up a whole new world of possibilities.*

Coincidence? Perhaps not!
These are just few of the synchronistic true stories I found while doing research online. There were hundreds more.

Twin Boys, twin lives-

The stories of identical twins living nearly identical lives are often astonishing, but perhaps none more so than those of identical twins born in Ohio. The twin boys were separated at birth, being adopted by different families. Unknown to each other, both families named the boys James. And here the coincidences just begin. Both Jameses grew up not even knowing of the other, yet both sought law-enforcement training, both had abilities in mechanical drawing and carpentry, and each had married women named Linda. They both had sons whom one named James Alan and the other named James Allan. The twin brothers also each divorced their first wives and married other women, both named Betty! And they both owned dogs that they named Toy. Forty years after their childhood separation, the two men were reunited to share their amazingly similar lives. (Reader's Digest, January 1980).

Laura Buxton, meet Laura Buxton-

In June 2001, Laura Buxton (almost 10) released a red balloon into the air over her hometown of Stoke-on-Trent in Staffordshire, England. On one side of the balloon, she had written "Please return to Laura Buxton," and on the other side, her home address. A few weeks later, a man 140 miles away in Milton Lilbourne found the balloon stuck in the hedge that separated his farm from the next-door neighbor's. He noticed Laura Buxton's name and address and immediately took the balloon to the neighbor's house showing it to the 10-year-old girl who lived there ... whose name was also Laura Buxton!

Laura Buxton from Milton Lilbourne wrote to Laura Buxton from Stoke-on-Trent to let her know that she'd found the balloon. Thinking this coincidence was simply too amazing to be true, they decided they had to meet in person. And that's when things got really weird.

On the day of the meeting, the two girls wore essentially the same outfit – a pink sweater and jeans. The girls were the same height, which was unusual because they were both tall for their age. They both had brown hair and wore it in the same style. They both had three-year-old black Labrador retrievers at home, as well as gray pet rabbits. They both brought their guinea pigs, which were the same color and even had the same orange markings on their hindquarters. It was almost as though these two Laura Buxtons were the same person.

The strange events surrounding their meeting helped the girls form a strong bond. Both felt the circumstances that brought them together were too significant to write off as mere coincidence. For more on the Lauras, listen to this 2009 RadioLab interview- radiolab.org/2009/jun/15/a-very-lucky-wind.

(Source: *Mental Floss Magazine*, March, 2011 written by Rob Lammle)

A book by any other name…

The British actor Anthony Hopkins was delighted to hear that he had landed a leading role in a film based on the book The Girl From Petrovka, by George Feifer. A few days after signing the contract, Hopkins travelled to London to buy a copy of the book. He tried several bookshops, but there wasn't one to be had. Waiting at Leicester Square underground for his train home, he noticed a book apparently discarded on a bench. Incredibly, it was The Girl From Petrovka.

That in itself would have been coincidence enough but in fact it was merely the beginning of an extraordinary chain of events. Two years later, in the middle of filming in Vienna, Hopkins was visited by George Feifer, the author. Feifer mentioned that he did not have a copy of his own book. He had lent the last one--containing his own annotations--to a friend who had lost it somewhere in London. With mounting astonishment, Hopkins handed Feifer the book he had found. "Is this the one?'" he asked, "with the notes scribbled in the margins?" It was the same book.

(Source: *2spare.com*)

I don't remember a time when I wasn't aware of synchronicities in my own life. When I was younger, I would say to my mom, "I think I make things happen." She would ask me what I meant, and I would tell her all kinds of "coincidences" that I later discovered were synchronicities. Since then, I have learned that when I pay attention to those synchronicities, they can support me in so many ways.

A few personal synchronicities:

Life is but a dream 1-

When my brother and I were young, we would share dreams. I'm not talking about simple little things that were similar about each other's dreams. I would wake up and remember I had seen him in my dream doing a certain thing, like riding a skateboard or running through a park, and I would ask him the next day if he remembered seeing me in his dream, and he would say, "Yeah, I waved at you as I was running through the park," or "Of course, we talked to each other when I was on my skateboard, and you were on your bike," The more we would talk about it as kids, the more in sync our dreams would become. Some might write it off as something we made up or talked ourselves into, yet because it was only one of many synchronistic things that happened to me as a kid, I knew it was more than that.

Life is but a dream 2-

I woke up from a nap in the middle of a Saturday afternoon crying from a dream I had. The dream was about a friend's older brother getting into a car accident and dying. I called my friend, hysterically sobbing, and told her about the dream. She put her brother on the phone and I begged him to 'please be careful, and wear his seat belt if he went anywhere that day' (he usually never wore his seat belt). He told me I was being silly and he would consider it. I told him his sister and I would follow him around everywhere if he didn't promise to do it. I even asked him to take us with him to the mall so I could be sure he would wear his seat belt. He thought I was just trying to get him to take us to the mall, but I was so sure it would change the dream if I was there with him. So, we went to the mall, and everything was fine. He did not get into an accident... until the next day!

I got a phone call the following day from him. He had just been in a car accident, which would have killed him if he had not put on his seat belt! He said he only wore it because he heard my voice in his head make him promise he would. According to the police at the scene, it saved his life.

A Pipe's Journey-

When I was early in my study along the path of the Lakota Tradition, I was called to work with a teacher (I call him my Uncle) who supports me on my journey. We discussed whether or not I would work with a Prayer Pipe, and I was really not sure. I decided to go on a Vision Quest to help me on my journey. My Uncle shared with me the many things I would need to do to prepare, and he let me know it would be a year-long preparation process. One thing he asked me to do was pray to know if I was meant to carry a Pipe. So I did. I prayed, I prepared, and I listened.

As the days got closer and closer to my Vision Quest, I figured maybe I was not meant to carry a Pipe since one had not made its way to me. Then one day, my best friend came to me and shared with me that she had been gifted a Prayer Pipe by her mother-in-law who had recently passed away. My friend thought I already had a Pipe, so when she contacted me, she did not know I was still wondering if I was meant to have one. She knew (for several reasons) that this Pipe was not for her, she could not understand why she felt so strongly called to give it to me 'since I already had one', and she just 'knew' that Pipe was mine. I did my Vision Quest with that Pipe, and it is the Pipe I pray with to this day.

There are many moments in life when we are given clues and guidance by what I consider to be the 'Inner Voice.' Synchronicities show up to lead us along a path, and I find that when I do *truly listen* to my Inner Voice, I am guided in ways I could not have made up or imagined. I am personally grateful for synchronicities. I believe they help make life so much more interesting, fascinating and fun.

> **NOTE/SUGGESTION:** *At the end of each day write in your journal at least two things that happened during the day that seemed like a "coincidence." Pay attention to how those "coincidences" may already be guiding your path. As you make a habit of paying attention, you will notice them more often, and they become even more supportive of your journey. It is as if you are telling the Universe how you prefer to receive information. The more you learn from and trust synchronicities, the more they will show up to support you!*

7) Gratitude and Planting "Seeds"

I love to practice gratitude at night before I go to bed. I have a stone that says "Gratitude" on it, and I hold it while I whisper to myself what I am grateful for from that day. Then I kiss the stone and set it aside. Next, I hold onto a small, white, marble, egg-shaped stone and I whisper to the stone a new "seed" or idea I would like to plant into my subconscious.

At first, it seemed like this exercise was something I did just because I liked the idea of it, and it felt good. And then, one morning, I woke up with the most awesome insight based on the "seed" I had planted the night before! Ever since then, the gratitude and seed planting practice is an ongoing favorite. It feels good to create new ideas and opportunities to become open to. The seed planting idea has even given me the inspiration for another book I am writing!

I suggest adding night-time gratitude and seed planting to whatever daily or weekly gratitude you may already be practicing.

Caterpillar Stage Conclusion:

To conclude the Caterpillar Stage, the two most important things to remember are: **1) try new things**, and **2) pay attention**. The more open you are to new things, the more open you will be to step through your fears and into that which you want to have, experience, be, or do in your life.

This is the stage where you are able to test your limiting personal boundaries and move beyond them. It is the stage where you are given permission to start *re-creating yourself*.

As you move beyond this stage, be willing to continue creating and allowing new opportunities for yourself to evolve. Be gentle, yet also be willing to push your personal boundaries to learn more about yourself. Notice synchronicities, be grateful, try new things, and be inspired and inspiring. There are no limits to the possibilities available to you.

The next stage is one where you can absorb the new things you have been learning about yourself and integrate them as a part of your ongoing life experience. Before you move on, first decide if you need more time in the Caterpillar Stage. If so, take some time to look at some of the more challenging tools and try them again. Journal and sit with what you have learned from the Caterpillar Stage tools and only *then* move on to the Cocoon Stage.

JOURNAL SECTION - Caterpillar Stage

The sacred moment came when the imaginal cells called forth what was to come next; full surrender into a cocoon, allowing for the growth needed for a greater, more vibrant expression of this, this delicate new life to begin. The caterpillar experienced a new found peace and trust in the cool darkness.

~Christine Ruddy

III. Cocoon Stage

"Follow effective action with quiet reflection. From the quiet reflection will come even more effective action."
~Peter F. Drucker

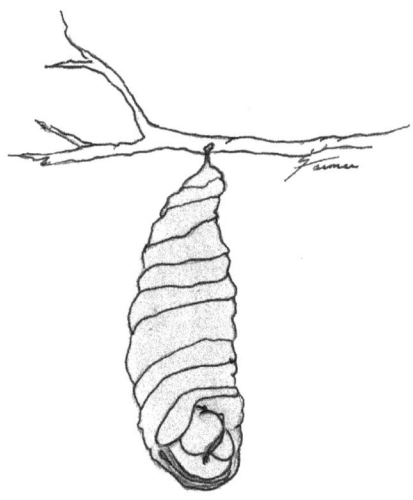

The Cocoon Stage is a time for reflection and contemplation on what you have learned from your journey so far. You may feel like taking some time for yourself to integrate the newness you are allowing in your life.

Cocoon Stage Main Focus:
Nurturing Integration

Integration (in the Merriam-Webster medical dictionary online) is defined as: *"the combining and coordinating of separate parts or elements into a unified whole."* I use the term integration here to describe how the many single bits and pieces of information gained through the first two stages can be combined together and absorbed more deeply during the Cocoon Stage to become a unified part of your new life experience.

To integrate new knowledge, information, awareness, or growth, you must take the time to **be quiet and reflect** on anything new that has just been introduced into your life. It is also important to **be very gentle and loving** with yourself through this delicate stage.

If you avoid taking the time to fully integrate new information, much of that information can be lost. By avoiding integration, you may be tempted to return to old "comfort zones," ending up somewhere close to where you started.

When you take the time to *stop* and allow the integration of new information to become a part of your field, you can avoid having to return repeatedly to the Egg Stage for the same issue.

There is a phenomenon about a caterpillar becoming a butterfly inside the cocoon whereby *imaginal cells* (Terms, p. 137) take over to create the butterfly. Science explains imaginal cells more specifically in a few article links found on p. 138.

I will explain it here in layperson's terms. When a caterpillar creates its cocoon, it carries its "old" caterpillar cells into the cocoon with it. It also carries with it imaginal cells or the "new" butterfly cells (which have actually always been around waiting to spring into action when the time was right, yet were previously unnecessary to the caterpillar). Once the breakdown of the caterpillar's molecular structure begins, it basically melts and becomes a sort of gooey liquid, which contains the caterpillar cells and the imaginal butterfly cells. The imaginal cells activate and start attacking the "old" caterpillar cells. For a little while, the "old" (tired) caterpillar cells put up a pretty good fight, yet eventually, the "new" (stronger) butterfly cells win, and those cells grow to become the butterfly ... In other words, within the cocoon, the caterpillar cells and the butterfly cells BOTH share the cocoon space for some time. At some point, the caterpillar cells must let go of being a caterpillar so that the butterfly cells can take over and create the butterfly.

Much like a caterpillar which enters its cocoon, *you* must be ready to let go of old patterns, expectations, and cellular memory to allow your own "imaginal cells" to take over and manifest as your new reality. This allowing takes a lot of trust in yourself and the choices you are making.

The Cocoon Stage is a crucial stage which provides tools and support to help you trust yourself and move forward to embrace the new you.

Chakras for the Cocoon Stage

> *The chakras you are working with in the Cocoon Stage are the 6th and 7th chakras. The Third Eye/Indigo, and the Crown/Violet chakras are the energy centers most deeply connected to Source/God/Universal Wisdom. Your trust, your "inner-guidance system," your intuition, your "psychic gifts," and your 'deeper knowing' are centered in these two upper chakras.*
>
> *By tuning in to the 6th and 7th chakras during this stage, you are allowing your connections to deepen and shift to support all the changes you have made in the first five (plus High-heart) chakras. You are letting your own inner guidance and your connection to Source know you are ready to make the changes in key areas of your energy field and your life.*

Cocoon Stage Check-In: Am I Capable?

Sit quietly and breathe. Check in with your inner guidance by tuning into your thoughts, your feelings, and your physical body. Write your answers and feelings in your journal or in this book. Ask yourself:

1) Do I feel good about where I am?

2) Do I feel overwhelmed by all the new information I have been taking in?

3) Am I ready for some time alone or quiet time away from my familiar/comfortable places (including my family, friends, job, school, etc.)?

4) Has something happened to force me to take some quiet time for myself (cold or flu, vacation, sabbatical from work or school, family out of town and me alone at home, something seemingly "out of my control" to force me to stop my normal routine)?

5) Am I ready to embrace and integrate all I have taken in through the Egg and Caterpillar Stages?

6) Am I nervous and/or excited about this stage?

7) Am I willing to do the work anyway?

8) Do I notice a newfound confidence I did not have before starting this process?

9) Am I willing to step into and accept my new life experiences?

If you answered yes to three or more of the above questions, you are most likely ready to step into the Cocoon Stage. This is a very reverent and deeply integrative place to be. The satisfaction may not, on the surface, seem as important as getting through the Egg Stage or the active Caterpillar Stage, but that is because the cocoon provides a time of quiet reflection, internal listening, and deep absorption of the new information you have been taking in.

Embrace the Cocoon Stage:

It is now time to find a place to spend a day to a few days alone, where you can **fully focus on yourself** throughout this stage. You might find there is some resistance from those around you and possibly even from yourself. Your spouse or partner, your workplace, your children, your parents, or your friends may try talking you out of taking this time for yourself. They may not be ready to let go of the you that they have become familiar with over the years. Change in you can sometimes create fear in those around you because, on some level, they are realizing that if you are changing, they may also need to look at their own lives more deeply.

Remember, *you* are the creator of change in *your* life. When you take on this process, you are saying YES to those changes. This acceptance of change requires courage and inner strength on your part. And remember, the main purpose for moving through this process is to get you *out* of any suffering mentality, and *into* your divine Bliss. *Only* when you are ready to step fully into your new life, *and* you have found a quiet place to integrate the new you, move on to the next section of this stage. By reading on, you are saying "yes" to embracing the changes you have been creating through the first half of this book. Changes WILL occur as you read on.

One of my favorite chants to support this stage is the following:

"I am opening up in sweet surrender
to the luminous love-light of the One."
~Flight of the Hawk

NOTE: *If any of the above seems confusing, try going back to the Egg and/or Caterpillar Stage and checking in with yourself. Have you fully prepared yourself to integrate what you have learned? OR, take some time to review your journal up to this point. Be sure you have allowed yourself to fully and gently move through the first two stages. If you have forced your way too quickly through the Egg or Caterpillar Stages, the Cocoon Stage could seem very frustrating or scary, and may not even make sense. Take some time to look at where you are right now. Be sure you are as complete with the first two stages as you can be at this time.*

Use this space to draw an egg, caterpillar, cocoon, butterfly, or any image that supports your journey. (Other suggestions: Swirls, stars, hearts, a tree, a poem, peace symbol, Ohm symbol, yin yang)

Affirmation for the Cocoon Stage:

Breathe in and out from your heart and say to yourself out loud:

"I am ready to allow all of the information received in the Egg and Caterpillar Stages to become integrated as the new me. I allow all old cellular memory which no longer serves me to fall away, and I allow the new ideas and tools I have been working with to take their place as my NOW reality. I am open and receptive to the New Me."

Tools for the Cocoon Stage:

- *Notes for this stage can be made on pp. 103-106.*
- *You can add your own tools for this stage on p. 141.*
- *Draw "Tools" into your toolbox below.*
- *Creative Suggestion: Gather your favorite cuddly slippers, stuffed animal, PJs, blanket, or other comfort "tools" to use throughout your personal reflective time.*

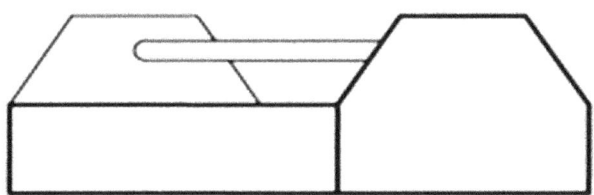

1) Nurturing Retreats or Workshops (p. 90)
2) Massage, Acupuncture, Other Energy Work (p. 92)
3) Nurturing Movies (p. 93)
4) Integrative Baths (p. 94)
5) "One for One at 1:00" (p. 95)
6) Fasts/Cleanses (p. 96)
7) Clearing Your Environment (p. 97)
8) Divination Cards (p. 98)
9) Shaman-Led Experiences (p. 99)
10) Gratitude and Dream Journal (p. 101)

Below are descriptions of The Cocoon Stage Tools *and some suggestions for using them in your day-to-day life, as well as information on how to learn more about them. Be sure to use your journal or the journal pages in this book to write down any notes, thoughts, and feelings as you move through this stage.*

1) <u>Nurturing Retreat or Workshop, Reflection Time</u>

There are so many places to retreat to for nurturing, loving, and caring self-time. Try hot springs, a week-long or weekend silent workshop, a retreat center, a spa, a friend's empty summer home, a cabin in the woods, or some other quiet place where you can take time for yourself, uninterrupted by everyday concerns and activities.

When you find a place that suits your needs and desires, do yourself a favor and include a massage or other energy session such as Reiki, Breema, acupuncture or other energy support. Many retreat centers, workshops, shamans, and healers, can support you with deep integration tools such as:

- *Tai Chi/Yoga*

From *whatisholistic.com*: *"Tai Chi is a traditional Chinese mind-body relaxation exercise consisting of 108 intricate exercise sequences [plus meditation] performed in a slow relaxed manner over a 30 minute period. It may calm the nerves, tone muscles, and balance one's internal energy. In addition, the regular practice of Tai Chi may even slow down the aging process, help one to maintain agility, and promote and enhance the internal functions of the body. This low impact exercise can be done anywhere as it requires no equipment or special clothing."*

To find classes and more information on tai chi and its benefits, search online, check with your local health spa, health food store, food co-op, the library, or your local Community Center.

See the Egg Stage, p. 47, for a refresher on information about Yoga.

- *Drumming*

From *about.com*: "*The pounding sound of a drum can help us take notice of our own heartbeat, which keeps us alive and vital. Drumming can be very therapeutic in getting us in touch with our inner-self. A low, steady beat can create calmness whereas a strong upbeat can stir us into action.*"

Drumming is very relaxing, grounding, and centering to do by yourself or with a group. It can help you become very centered and support you in tuning in more deeply to the heartbeat of Mother Earth. It has been said that drums have been found in every ancient tribal society around the world, even though there was never any (known) communication between them. What this tells me is that there must be something inherent in the body and mind that completely tunes in to the sound and feel of a drum.

You can look up more information online, or at the library, about therapeutic drumming, healing drumming, drumming for health, and drum circles in your area.

• *Meditation*

"Meditation is to be still, to sit still, to stand still, and to walk with stillness. Meditation means to look deeply, to touch deeply so we can realize we are already home. Our home is available right here and right now."
~Thich Nhat Hanh

Some popular types of meditation you may encounter during a retreat or workshop, or a meditation/retreat/healing center may include mindfulness, yoga nidra, transcendental (TM), trance, tantric, religious, heart-centered, inclusive, dualistic, awakening, and many more.

See the Egg Stage, p.46, for more meditation information.

And remember, do not practice meditation while driving or doing anything else that would require your full attention!

2) <u>Massage, Acupuncture, and Other Energy Work</u>

All of the following forms of support include you lying down or sitting comfortably and receiving some form of physical or energetic support from a licensed or certified practitioner.

The following are some (but not all) forms of energy and healing support you can receive from an expert:

Massage, Reiki, Breema, Rolfing, Touch For Health, EFT/Tapping, Acupuncture, Chiropractic, Rosen Method, Aura and Chakra work, Sound

Healing, Reflexology, Energy Balancing, Craniosacral, Vibrational Medicine, Light Healing, Kinesiology, Ayurveda, Qi Gong, and many more.

Any energy that builds up over time in your body can accumulate and create a toxic environment that can often be difficult to clear out on your own. Having a session with someone who knows how to support you in releasing the stuck energy can be very healing and powerful. In case you have never had any of the above mentioned energy work before, do some research and see which one fits your personal style.

Be sure to drink a lot of water before and after any energy or physical bodywork session. Water helps clear out any toxins that can get released into your bloodstream during a session. I always feel so supported, nurtured, and clear after having any of this kind of work done.

To find a practitioner near you, look online, on the community board at your local health food center or healing bookstore, any New Thought Center, such as Unity or Centers For Spiritual Living, or ask around for references from trusted colleagues and friends. Even when I am not sure about trying something new, if I feel called to do it, I trust my inner guidance and try it anyway—always with good or great results.

3) <u>Nurturing Movies</u>

Below is a list of a few of my favorite "movies for integration" that I love to watch when I am in this stage of transformation. I love to vege out in front of a really life-affirming movie with some tea and a cozy blanket, allowing myself to integrate whatever might be otherwise difficult to think about or move through.

Many times I have received deep insight during or after a movie like this because I have allowed myself to open up and simply relax. Support and insight often shows up in my dreams after I have watched a particularly relaxing movie. I like to keep a journal with me throughout the Cocoon Stage just so I can record such events and insights.

During the Cocoon Stage, I recommend watching movies you do not have to "think" about while watching. I love most spiritual movies, but the ones that make you think (such as the ones listed on p. 68 in the Caterpillar Stage) are a little too "heady" for the Cocoon Stage. In this Stage you want to relax, not study or "think" too much.

I suggest joining Spiritual Cinema Circle. It is a great site that sends you spiritual movies every month for a low cost. Visit *spiritualcinemacircle.com*, or join some other movie club such as Netflix, Hulu Plus, Blockbuster, or Amazon Prime online.

Here is a list of some of my favorite, sweet, vege out, integration movies:

The Man From Earth, Serendipity, What Dreams May Come, Dan in Real Life, The Bucket List, Field Of Dreams, Groundhog Day, Déjà Vu, Evan Almighty, Bruce Almighty, Pay It Forward, The Princess Bride, The Blind Side, Wall-E, (just about ANY Disney, Pixar or other children's movies), *Cocoon, Chocolat, Like Water For Chocolate, The Last Mimzy, Bridge To Terabithia, August Rush, Avatar, 50 First Dates...*

And there are so many more! What are some of your favorites? Write them in the journal section of this stage, and please post them on my Butterfly Process Facebook page at *facebook.com/TheButterflyProcess*.

4) <u>Integrative Baths</u>

Bathing, soaking, sweating, and all forms of immersion in water are very helpful and often crucial during this time. As stated earlier, for a butterfly or moth during the Cocoon Stage, there is a melt-down process the caterpillar goes through. The caterpillar virtually turns into a liquid state, thus changing everything about the structure of the DNA, the form, and the being it once was. After the melt-down stage, what once was a caterpillar slowly becomes a butterfly (see pp. 85, 137 and 138 for more about the melt-down process of the caterpillar in the cocoon).

Time in the cocoon is a very delicate and fragile time. It is very important to be gentle with yourself and love yourself through this stage.

When you take baths during this Stage, keep it simple. If you decide to use scents or candles, keep it to one light scent, and be sure the candles are unscented. Avoid overdoing your experience in this stage. You are integrating many new things into your field, so you do not want to distract it with too much stimulus around you. Use this time to relax, unwind, and tune in to yourself and Source within.

If you decide to enjoy a steam room, bathhouse, hot tub, sauna, hot springs, etc., try to avoid the places where there is a lot of talking and action. Keep your communication to a minimum. This is YOUR TIME. Even create this time as a "no talking" time if you can. Take care of yourself and be as safeguarded and quiet as possible so you can allow all of the new experiences and lessons from the Egg and Caterpillar Stages to soak in and become a part of the new field ("the new DNA") you are creating for yourself.

5) <u>One for ONE at 1:00 Practice</u>

Take one minute for ONEness at 1:00 Daily
www.ONEnessDaily.com

As we all choose to remember Oneness, we are brought together in closer alignment with all beings on the planet. A good friend, Laura "Leela Vox" Alexander created the website: ONE*ness*Daily.com. Please check it out on the web and on Facebook to learn more.

Set your watch, phone, or some other alarm to go off at 1:00 p.m. (local time) every day, and ask others to do the same. When your alarm goes off at 1:00 p.m., take one minute to connect to your inner space and tune into Oneness. Breathe in and out through your heart and high-heart and think of something you are grateful for. See and feel your gratitude move out to everything and everyone, and allow the energy of Oneness and connection to engulf your field and become a part of your energy for the rest of the day.

During this time, if you can, close your eyes and step away from any distractions. Allow the peaceful moment of grace and deep cleansing breaths to fill your field with a sense of connection to the All. And, if you are driving or otherwise occupied, simply think about Oneness and your connection to all things with each cleansing breath.

6) Fasting/Cleansing

Before you decide to do a fast or cleanse, I recommend you speak with a professional such as a dietitian, a nutritionist, or a person who has done them and supported others in doing them successfully many times before striking out on your own.

Fasting and cleansing are helpful tools to support you in letting go of toxic waste and built-up energy in your blood, gall bladder, liver, kidneys, lymph, intestines, and other organs. Many different types of cleanses can support you in letting go at the deepest physical level, and thus allow any emotional waste or debris to loosen up and be released as well. There are many types of fasts and cleanses you can do.

Here are a few of my personal favorites:

- A juice fast
- A raw food fast
- The Chocolate Fast (book by Stasia Bliss)
- The Master Cleanse (*themastercleanse.org*)
- Specific organ cleanses (liver, gall bladder, kidney, lungs, intestines, blood, etc.)
- Liquid Feast (a specific type of supported liquid eating process to cleanse and nourish the body) – For more information, do a search for "Liquid Feast" online.

If you choose fasting or cleansing as a way to help you clear out the old and allow space for new energy in your life, please consult someone who knows how to support you through it. If you do not know what you are doing, you could cleanse too fast, dehydrate, and even throw off your metabolism or electrolyte balance. I highly recommend working with a health practitioner or expert the first few times you do a cleanse or fast.

7) <u>Feng Shui/Clearing Your Environment</u>

When you are doing a physical, body fast or cleanse of any kind, it is also a good idea to cleanse and clear your personal environment. You are creating more internal flow within your body, and it makes sense to do the same for your home, office, vehicle, and other areas you spend time in.

Look into using a feng shui professional, a personal organizer, or using books on those subjects to help support the flow of energy in your surroundings. There are many books, professionals, videos, and DVDs to support you in working with the flow of energy in and around your home and life.

Here are a few simple feng shui tips to do in any place you spend an extended amount of time:

o Think like the animals. Animals don't "poop where they sleep or eat," and it helps to have the same rule in your home. Do not put animal litter boxes in or around where you eat, sleep, or spend a lot of time in your daily life. Especially keep bathroom doors and toilet lids closed that are in or near your bedrooms, living areas, kitchen or dining room.

o "Soften" pointed or jagged areas and walls jutting out which point toward the places where you sleep, eat, work, or spend a lot of time—to avoid receiving what feng shui considers "killing arrows" into your field, disturbing your peaceful environment. If there are places where those pointy places cannot be changed or removed, hang a feng shui crystal ball, wind chimes, or some kind of flowy material over those edges so they dampen, break-up, or soften the "killing arrows."

- Have some kind of altar(s) set up in a prominent place(s). Keep this area free of clutter at all times. This space can help create flow in your home, office or other place you spend a lot of time. Use items you have collected and love. Keep crystals, a fountain, music instruments, a sand garden, candles, incense, or other sacred items in this area. Use the altar area for a place to meditate if you choose. This will also create and help maintain a peaceful, relaxed, and supportive environment within your home or office.

- Use sage, incense, sound, musical instruments, clap, snap, sing, yell, or use any other kind of clearing tools to break up the dense energy that can build up in your environment. Certain Native American tribes, traditional eastern cultures, and many religious groups use some form of clearing to shake up, release, loosen, and cleanse dense or negative energy. It supports your surroundings to stay open, clear, and free flowing.

- The most important thing to remember here is FLOW. The more the energy in your personal space flows, the more it will also flow in your body's own energy field.

8) Divination Cards

I love to use card decks for support and guidance. Many people call them tarot cards, oracle decks, or divination cards. I use them to support me in deepening a thought or idea. When I do not have another person to talk through something with, I often pull cards to gain some clarity, guidance, or support.

I fully embrace the use of therapists, practitioners, friends and others for support and guidance, and I also know that my own inner guidance system can support me. Sometimes, however, I know I can block myself from clarity about a particular situation or pattern. The cards are, in a way, an extension of my own inner voice. When I ask the deck a question and then pull a card, the answer is always insightful and supportive.

You can find many card decks through Hay House Publishing, *amazon.com*, or at any bookstore, spiritual center, or New Age book store or crystal shop.

Some of my favorite decks:
- *Path of the Soul Destiny Cards,* Cheryl Lee Hanish
- *Fairies Oracle,* Brian Froud and Jessica MacBeth
- *Inner Child Cards,* Isha Lerner and Mark Lerner
- *Medicine Cards,* Jamie Sams & David Carson
- *Ask Your Guides Oracle Deck,* Sonia Choquette
- *Angel, Goddess,* and *Ascended Masters Oracle Cards,* Doreen Virtue
- Any of Louise L. Hay's card decks
- *The Four Agreements Cards,* Don Miguel Ruiz
- *I Ching of The Goddess,* Barbara G. Walker
- *Archetype Cards,* Caroline Myss
- *Healing Cards,* Caroline Myss and Peter Occhiogrosso
- *MotherPeace,* Karen Vogel and Vicki Noble

9) Shaman-Led Experiences

- *Sweat Lodge*

From *crystalinks.com*: "*The sweat lodge (also called purification ceremony, sweat house, medicine lodge, medicine house, Inipi, or simply 'sweat') is a ceremonial sauna and is an important way of life for some North American First Nations or Native American cultures. There are several styles of sweat lodges that include a domed or oblong hut similar to a wickiup, or even a simple hole dug into the ground and covered with planks or tree trunks. Stones are typically heated in an exterior fire and then placed in a central pit in the ground.*"

Sweat lodge is a very sacred ceremonial way to sweat your prayers. This is something you will want to do with a shaman or other ceremonial teacher who can guide you through it. Many people offer sweat lodge, but not all are in the highest integrity. Once you decide you would like to participate in a sweat, you will be guided to the places you need to go to find the best teacher/shaman for you. It is not usually something you can look up online. Trust your guidance, especially from friends who have had this experience. And most importantly, be sure you feel safe and supported when you decide to participate in a sweat lodge ceremony.

- *Soul Retrieval*

From *themystica.com*: "*Soul retrieval is a shamanic skill used to heal a person from illness. Shamans believe that all illness comes from losing power or giving power away to something or someone … It may be a living being who has an energetic cord attached to you and is sucking part of your soul away. It can be a generational soul loss that happened many years ago with your grandfather or great-grandmother that you are not even aware of that has taken away part of your family soul. Soul loss can also be caused by a traumatic experience, a car accident, a sudden death in the family, a violent crime, or a chronic illness. These things can cause a loss of vital power or energy, and* (according to certain traditions) *that power and energy (a part of one's wholeness) must be restored to bring health and healing of body, mind and spirit back to the* [client]."

Be sure, if you choose to do a Soul Retrieval, that you find a shaman or other person who is skilled and trained in doing this work. You may have to ask around to trusted sources to find the best practitioner/shaman for you. Trust your gut.

Some places you could search: Wellness centers, spiritual centers, New Thought communities, or New Age/metaphysical shops.

- *Journeying*

A great website that defines and explains journeying and its many benefits is: *shamanlinks.net/journey.htm*

Quoted from this site: "*Journeying, like meditation, is a tool for spiritual growth. It is also a tool that can be used for healing, obtaining information, and working through psychological issues. When someone goes on a 'journey,' they are able to communicate on a spiritual level. So they can go and visit guardian spirits, they can go and visit spirits of the land. A journeyer can use a journey to examine the health of their body or another's body. They can also discover things about the world.*"

I am simply going to repeat what I wrote above: Be sure, if you choose to try journeying, that you find a shaman, a sacred or traditional medicine person, or other person who is skilled and trained in doing this kind of work. You may have to ask around to trusted sources to find the best practitioner/shaman for you. Trust your gut.

Some places you could search: Wellness centers, spiritual centers, New Thought communities, or New Age/metaphysical shops.

10) <u>Gratitude and Dream Journal</u>

I have combined two of my favorite kinds of journals to keep it simple during this time of integration. Instead of writing your thoughts in a regular journal, try this for a while:

1) Keep a journal next to your bed and write five things you are grateful for at the end of every day.

2) When you wake up, write about your dreams in the same journal.

Some things you may start to notice:

- Experiences in your life seem to line up more.
- Synchronicities may connect your dreams to your gratitudes each day.
- Your dreams may support and guide you more clearly.
- It may become difficult to write only five things in your gratitude journal each day!

Cocoon Stage Conclusion:

To conclude this stage, remember the most important thing you have been doing through this stage is allowing your integration process to happen *gently*.

Being quiet, and reflecting on all you have learned through the first two stages is essential in this Stage. Did you support yourself by **being gentle and loving** as you allowed the "new you" to be lovingly birthed into the world?

Taking the time to truly nurture and gently support yourself through this stage of integration is key to unlocking the next step of your evolution.

Be sure you are complete with the Cocoon Stage before diving into the Butterfly Stage. You have done so much work up to this point, and you definitely want to feel supported and ready before stepping into the last Stage of *The Butterfly Process*.

Check in with yourself. Are you feeling integrated? Do you feel supported and ready to move to the next Stage? Do you feel safe? Are you giving yourself plenty of time to breathe and tune in with your energy? If the answer to those questions is yes, then get ready to move on to the Butterfly Stage. If you are not quite ready, take a moment to meditate or use a favorite tool from one of the prior Stages, or one you created for yourself. Give yourself *the time you need* to prepare for the evolution of your Personal Transformation Journey.

Now, get ready to fly!

JOURNAL SECTION - Cocoon Stage

IV. Butterfly Stage

*"What the caterpillar calls the end of the world,
the master calls a butterfly."
~Richard Bach*

Ahhhh, the Butterfly Stage ... You are almost complete with this particular journey. There are only a few more steps to do. Prepare to spread your wings and fly, sweet Butterfly!

Butterfly Stage Main Focus:

Presence and Integrity

So far, you have:
- Opened yourself to new possibilities
- Stepped into and embraced change
- Taken the time to read, learn, study, and try new things
- Gotten quiet, gentle, and loving with yourself
- Reflected on what you have learned about the new, empowered life you are creating for yourself

Now it is time for the Butterfly Stage! Time to allow yourself (as much as possible!) to let go of what has not been working in your life, take a leap of faith, and step into the unknown. Coming out of the cocoon might feel a little scary, yet, it can also be one of the most empowering, exciting, necessary steps you have ever taken!

In this stage, the key is to **follow through** on your personal commitment to *face and embrace* your life with your full presence and integrity.

Chakras for the Butterfly Stage

In this stage, you are using and connecting to ALL of your chakras! Up to now, you have been working on individual chakras and small groups of chakras. Now, all of the chakras come together to support the life you have been preparing yourself for.

During this stage, your chakras will be aligning and tuning in to each other so they can work together to support you as a whole chakra system. This alignment and support will emanate from you, into the energy field that surrounds you, and out into the world AS YOU!

Butterfly Stage Check-In:
Taking Responsibility!

This is another good time to check in with yourself and be sure you are feeling fully supported, integrated, excited, and empowered.

Take note, in this stage (similar to the Egg Stage), you may find yourself becoming mildly emotional, irritable, easy to anger or fall into tears. Simply do your best to stay present. You will get through this by remaining patient, gentle, loving, and kind with yourself. Plus, remember, you can always use your favorite tools from the previous stages to support you.

By saying "yes" in each of the former stages, you have made it clear to yourself and those who support you that you are ready to fully embrace your new, empowered life!

And, just what does that mean, "new, empowered life"? Well, stepping onto your path of purpose and passion involves stepping out of the comfort zones you have created over the years. Comfort zones that *seem* to keep you safe and protected, yet can also keep you trapped in the familiar and mundane. Some people may enjoy that kind of life, but I say, why not *evolve* and be the best *You* that you can be by opening your heart and mind to *all* you are capable of?

Once you step onto the path of your personal evolution, (meaning evolution of your emotional life, experiences, connection with Source, physical body, mind, heart, friends, financial situations, career, etc.) you are saying "yes" to the life you desire. You are saying, "I am done with following the 'status quo' simply because it is comfortable for everyone else." And, "I am ready to live my life for ME!" New possibilities will "coincidentally" begin to enter your life like this or another book, a person to offer guidance and support, a class, a new job, a new friendship, or a new relationship.

You are creating your life all the time whether you are doing so consciously or not. Whatever you were thinking about last week, last month, or last year is what is becoming manifest as the life you are living today. When you decide to change your thoughts to support the life you desire to live, you must be strong and courageous, and step away from the naysayers who will try anything to keep you in the comfortable, mundane, "normal" life *they* are accustomed to in relationship with you.

> **NOTE**: *Although some people may try to stop your process as you choose to make major life changes, they do not do this to <u>keep</u> you from your goals and desires. Changes in you may lead them to look more deeply at themselves in ways for which they are not ready.*
>
> *Continue to move toward your transformation goals anyway. What others think about you (or even try to blame on you) is none of your business, is nothing personal, and actually has nothing to do with you. It's their own stuff, and they must deal with it in their own way.*

So often, people choose to stay in situations that do not serve or fulfill their personal desires and goals, or their creative hearts and minds, because they do not want to "hurt someone else's feelings." Choosing to stay in a certain place for another person is choosing to live dependent upon the other person's feelings and desires. The term most often used for this kind of pattern is "co-dependency." This co-dependent living is what keeps people in unhappy, long-term experiences (jobs, relationships, family situations, etc.) that do not serve or support the best and highest possibilities for their lives.

And just to be clear, I am NOT - *by any means* - saying leave your family, your job, or all that you are experiencing in your life right now. No. What I AM saying is this: When you are ready to step into your most empowered life, you are ready to take your life into your *own* hands. You are ready to live it from *your* inner guidance, *your* high-heart, and *your* "inner driver." You are no longer willing to allow others to drive (guide) your vehicle (body/soul/personal choices) through life. *You become the driver of your life*! That is what an empowered life can look like.

Something else to be aware of: When you start saying "yes" to your inner driver, you may be challenged by situations which might seemingly try to slow your progress. These challenges are often your ego holding on, or old *pain-bodies* (Terms p. 137) fighting to protect you from any major changes. Just remember, the ego/pain-bodies do not have any power over you unless you give it to them. Gently, calmly moving through them is simply one more step toward claiming, embracing, and accepting your empowered life!

The more you face and release your pain-bodies, the less difficult it becomes. The first step is often the hardest. Once you are willing to take that first step out of your comfort zones, and start saying *"yes"* to what you desire, each subsequent time becomes noticeably easier.

Use this space to add your own butterflies.

Embrace the Butterfly Stage:

The Butterfly Stage is a culminating opportunity for rejoicing in and embracing your life, and **being fully present**. It is also the stage for **pure, personal, unadulterated honesty and authenticity**. This Stage offers you the opportunity to decide if you are truly willing to face and move through all adversity to reach the final goal of "lifting off" into your new life.

While this is the Stage you have been working toward, you may be surprised at how much more there is yet to do to complete your journey. Do not let this distract you from attaining your goal of completion; you are in the homestretch now!

NOTE: *Possible Challenges*

When you are in this stage coming out of the cocoon and learning to live as a butterfly, some big challenges may surface for you to face, deal with, or move through. Those challenges could include:

- *Your former life enticing you to change your mind and come back to your old patterns, comfort zones, "safety," etc.*
- *People in your life asking challenging questions for you to "prove" you know what you are doing. (The fact is, you do not know exactly what you are doing yet. AND, it is not up to you to prove yourself to others just so they can understand, feel comfortable with, or accept your choices.)*
- *Getting caught up in other people's challenging questions, hurts, frustrations, or fears (co-dependency creeping back in).*
- *Your own inner voices trying to hold on to comfortable routines and patterns. (This may show up as inner struggle, anxiety, fear-based thoughts, or the feeling of "too much to do.")*

If these or any other issues surface and seemingly cause you to become paralyzed, simply take a moment, stand firm, and breathe into your heart. Then go back to any of the notes you have written in previous chapters, or your journal, and remember why you made the choice to go through this process in the first place. Whatever challenges you are meant to face in this stage, you have built up a new suit of courage to face them, move through them, and become stronger.

You may again find yourself asking, "Is it really worth it to take these steps, release old patterns, and make these changes?" As an experiment, I suggest that you ask anyone who has done something you consider important, new, awesome, or extreme in the world (it could be a teacher, a friend, an elder, or anyone else you look up to) about the challenges they faced to get where they are today. I would be willing to wager they will smile and say, "It was not easy, yet it was *all* worth it."

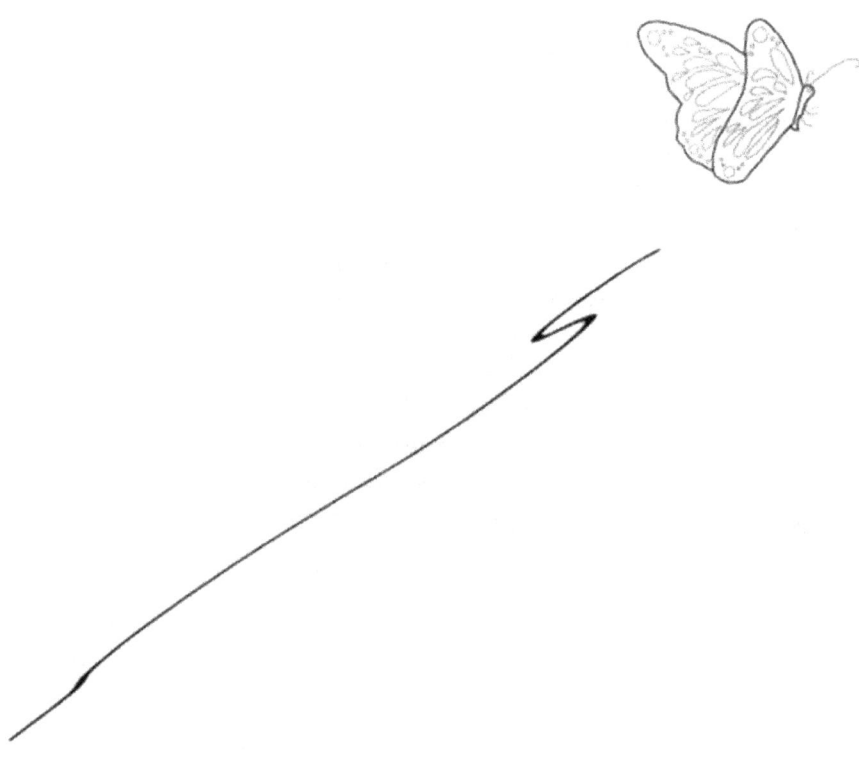

Affirmation for the Butterfly Stage:

Breathe in and out from your heart and say to yourself out loud:

"I am now ready to take flight and live as the true, perfect, beautiful butterfly that has always been my greatest possibility. I now embrace my soul's purpose, and I allow myself to live my passion and share my gifts and talents with the world. My life's purpose is already within me, and I am deeply committed to its unfoldment. In this and every moment, I AM FREE TO BE ME!"

A mantra you can use to support yourself through this stage might be: *"I am rooted; I am free; I am safe to be me. I am Spirit Divine; I am love; peace is mine"*

(Or make up a mantra for yourself!)

Tools for the Butterfly Stage:

- *Notes for this stage can be made on pp. 129-132.*
- *You can add your own tools for this stage on p. 142.*
- *Create "Tools" to put into your toolbox below.*
- *Creative Suggestion: Write your favorite tools on small pieces of paper and place them in a pouch or bag. Pull out a tool and use it when you feel the need for support.*

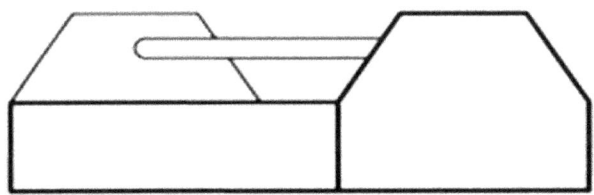

1) Choose A Healthy Lifestyle (p. 116)
2) Being Present (p. 117)
3) "Building Bridges" (p. 119)
4) Life Visioning (p. 124)
5) "GTG" (Go To Gratitude!) (p. 126)
6) Gather Your Tools (p. 127)

Below are descriptions of The Butterfly Stage Tools *and some suggestions for using them in your day-to-day life, as well as information on how to learn more about them. Be sure to use your journal or the journal pages in this book to write down any notes, thoughts, and feelings as you move through* The Butterfly Stage.

1) <u>Choose A Healthy Lifestyle</u>:
   o   Now is a great time to tune in to what you want to start doing more or less of to stabilize and strengthen your *physical and emotional health*.
   o   During the Butterfly Stage, you can really tune in, tune-up, and get your body's engines (organs, systems, bones, blood, health, etc.) running at their best. The Butterfly Stage is a great time to check in and *become present with what you need, what may be missing, or what you want more of in your life*. Now is the time to start doing, having, and experiencing them.
   o   If you have been putting off getting a checkup with your doctor, nutritionist, chiropractor, acupuncturist, dentist, etc., now is the time to do it! If you have wanted to change your diet or exercise routine, or to start one you have been drawn to, talk to a health care professional and do it! If you have been needing to get your eyes checked or prescription(s) changed, do it now!
   o   This is also a great time to change from your familiar *clothing and hairstyles* to new ones, which reflect the newly empowered *You*.

If you are not ready to change your entire wardrobe, at least go into your closet and dresser(s), pull out what you have not worn in the past 12 months and take them to a local homeless shelter. Then, go to a clothing store that sells used clothes and get yourself a few "new-to-you" things to support the new energy you are creating for yourself.

For the ladies, consider hosting a "Clothing Swap Party/Naked Lady Gathering." I call mine "Naked Goddess Gatherings" (I have suggested this idea to men too, and so far, only women have shown interest). Invite your girlfriends over and ask them to bring all the (clean) clothes, shoes, jewelry, etc. they no longer want. Put out snacks and, with curtains drawn and a few mirrors around, pile the clothes and shoes in the middle of the room (or in ordered piles around the room) so that each of you can find a new wardrobe!

No one has to spend any money, and your old clothes go to new homes (all "leftovers" can go to a women's shelter, kidney foundation, veterans organization, etc.). I have often walked away from these parties with a whole new wardrobe! The gatherings are great for season changes, weight changes, or when you have completed "The Butterfly Process" and are simply ready for visible change. Have fun with this!

2) <u>The Present is a Gift</u>

Awareness of the present moment is a conscious practice. Once you have practiced it for a while, you may notice how helpful it is in supporting your newly empowered life.

Awareness: 1) prevents you from dwelling on past experiences (which are no longer current or relevant); 2) prevents you from dwelling on potential future experiences (which may never happen, so are also irrelevant); and 3) supports you in living in the present moment, which is ALWAYS changing!

Following are some tools to support living in the now:

- *Affirm*

Post quotes and daily affirmations around your house. Here are some to get you started:

➢ *A planned future is a closed future. Allow yourself to dream and plan, but leave enough room for life to surprise you!* ~ Almine

➢ *Between shifting and allowing is surrendering to the moment* ~Terra Bundance

➢ *I expand in abundance, success, joy, peace, bliss, and love everyday as I inspire those around me to do the same.* ~ Gay Hendricks

➢ *Your hand opens and closes, opens and closes. If it were always a fist or always stretched open, you would be paralyzed. Your deepest presence is in every small contracting and expanding, the two as beautifully balanced and coordinated as birds' wings.* ~ Rumi

➢ *Trust that life is unfolding perfectly! Surrender to the moment* ~Terra Bundance

➢ *Be here now.* ~Ram Dass

➢ *Your true home is in the here and now.* ~Thich Nhat Hanh

- *Stay "Tuned"*

Read books, watch movies, and attend workshops and classes that support living in the present moment:

➢ *The One Thing Holding You Back*, book/classes/workshops, Raphael Cushnir, *cushnir.com*

➢ *A New Earth* and *The Power of Now*, Eckhart Tolle, *eckharttolle.com*

➢ *The Four Agreements, The Mastery of Love,* and *The Voice of Knowledge*, Don Miguel Ruiz, *miguelruiz.com*

➢ Abraham-Hicks books and workshops, *abraham-hicks.com*

➢ Oprah's Book Club has many great books about living in the moment, *oprah.com*

➢ Spiritual Cinema Circle distributes movies on presence and living in the moment, as well as other spiritual themes, *spiritualcinemacircle.com*

➢ Commercial movies such as: *50 First Dates, Groundhog Day, Stranger Than Fiction, Bruce Almighty, Evan Almighty, The Truman Show, Source Code, Big, Forrest Gump*, and others are great movies to support living in the moment.

- *Do It!*

Write that book, finish that CD, take that trip, start that company, follow through on things you have been saying you will do one day, spend time with friends or family you feel drawn to... NOW! Once you start doing everything you have been putting off, you will likely find yourself more present than you have ever been.

> *"Never put off 'til tomorrow what can be done today."*
> *~Thomas Jefferson*

Living life in "tomorrows" and "yesterdays" will steal your life in this moment away. Living in this moment will feed you in ways beyond your wildest imaginings. Give yourself the gift of presence; you are the *only* one who can!

3) <u>Building Bridges</u>

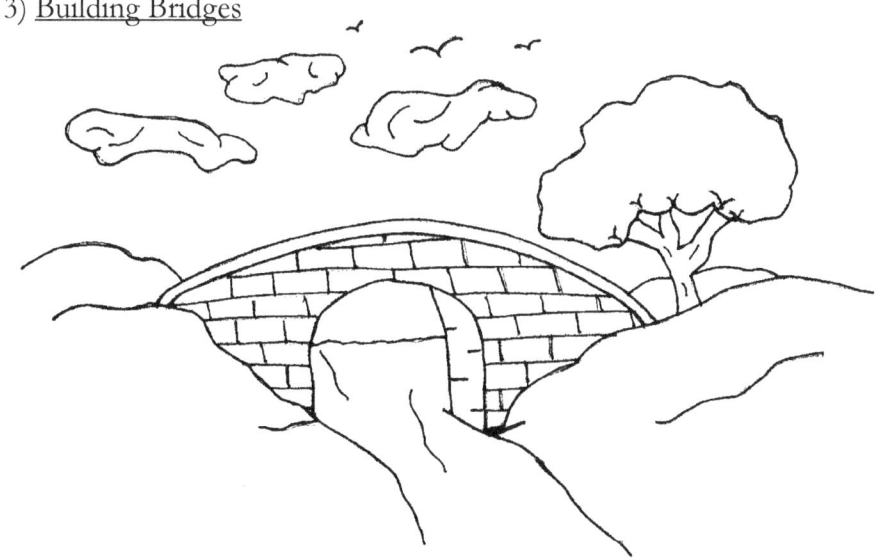

"Building Bridges" is a two-part concept that came to me through several meditations and dreams. The first part has to do with connecting to your own past to heal old wounds, concepts and beliefs, and the second part has to do with connecting in relationship with another person.

A) *Building Bridges with 'The Past'*

This concept came to me during a deep meditation I had. After practicing it a few times, I became aware that it is very similar to doing personal Soul Retrieval (as described on p. 100).

Often, when a traumatic, painful, or frightening experience happens in childhood, you might leave behind a "fragment" of yourself to protect the Child Self who experienced and still remembers the original trauma. I have created a meditation to support you in possibly unlocking, healing, and releasing those painful memories. The process calls on the Past Self and Future Self to heal the Child Self, and to reclaim the lost fragments from the past negative situations, resulting in a freer Present Self. This meditation can be used when you are ready to let go of any old beliefs or traumas from your childhood, from past lives, from family history, or any old patterns that no longer serve or support you.

To listen to me leading the Building Bridges meditation, please go to *terrabundance.com*, go to the meditation page, and find the link for "Building Bridges Meditation".

Before you start the meditation, be sure you are in a safe, comfortable environment with no distractions, and keep your journal next to you for any revelations that may come to you during or after the meditation. Please do not do the meditation while driving or doing any other strenuous activity.

NOTE: *This process can sometimes be very intense. You may choose to have someone you trust with you for support while you do the meditation.*

B) *Building Bridges in Relationships*

In every relationship, it is up to you to connect with the other person or people involved in the relationship, while still maintaining your own perspectives and boundaries. As a personally responsible human being, you are always building your side of every relationship you are in, while the other person is building their side. Sometimes, conflicts can arise if you try to change how the other person is building their side of the bridge, or if they try to change how you are building yours. "Building Bridges" is simply a concept or perspective, which allows space for each person in any relationship to be responsible for and maintain his or her own side of the bridge while allowing the space for the other person to do the same on their side of the bridge.

There are many books available that can support communication and connection in relationships. I will list a few of my favorites below. Although each of the books below has a slightly different focus on relationships than what I am discussing here, they all have supported me as I have been unraveling the mysteries of "Building Bridges" in relationships.

I suggest one or more of the following books to support you in better understanding your part/'your side of the bridge' in your relationships. These books can be helpful, but are not necessary to work with this tool.

- *Men Are From Mars, Women Are From Venus* by John Gray- "*A classic guide to understanding the opposite sex, (which) provides a practical and proven way for men and women to improve their communication by acknowledging the differences between their needs, desires, and behaviors*" (*Amazon.com*).
- *Nonviolent Communication* by Marshall Rosenberg- "*Nonviolent Communication (NVC) is sometimes referred to as compassionate communication. Its purpose is to: 1. create human connections that empower compassionate giving and receiving 2. create governmental and corporate structures that support compassionate giving and receiving*" (cnvc.org- The Center for Nonviolent Communication).
- *The 5 Love Languages* by Gary Chapman- "*The basic concept is that people communicate and feel love in different ways. Dr. Chapman has observed*

five different categories in which people communicate or understand love." (Christine Walker, *lifeloveandlogic.blogspot.com*).

Following are two hypothetical scenarios to show how we can better relate to one another while also maintaining our own side of the bridge:

1) "Sally" and "Ted" are in a business relationship, and they are working on a project together. This project has many layers, and both Ted and Sally are really excited about it. Sally starts working on her part of the project, while Ted starts working on his, and things move along smoothly. One day, Ted mostly completes his first part of the project and jumps to another part he knows he can work on. Sally continues to work on her first part of the project, slowly and steadily. Ted keeps jumping from one part of the project to another for a while. He mostly (but not completely) finishes each step until he stops one day and asks Sally why she is still working on her first part of the project. She says, "because I am allowing it to unfold naturally and completely before I go to the next part." Ted doesn't understand. Then Sally asks Ted why he isn't completing any of his steps before jumping to a new one. Ted says. "I already know how it will unfold; I simply have to do a little bit in each area for it all to come together." Sally doesn't understand.

Ted tries to help Sally with her part, but Sally doesn't need Ted's help; she has been doing really well with it on her own and knows that if her process becomes forced, it won't work properly. Sally starts telling Ted how to finish one of his projects, but Ted doesn't need Sally to tell him how to do it. He was working just fine without her help.

In the beginning, Sally was building her side of the bridge, and Ted was building his. They each know how to build their side of the bridge really well. They originally started working together because they each really appreciated the other's knowledge, ability and skill set for the project. The problem is, Ted started trying to build Sally's side of the bridge, and Sally started trying to build Ted's side.

Each side is equally important, and needs to run a certain way for the project to come together, but if they continue to mess around on each other's side of the bridge, it will become confusing and frustrating.

Sally's 'bricks' won't work or even fit correctly on Ted's side of the bridge, and vice versa. As soon as they each tried changing the way the other person was building their side of the bridge, not only did they stop the other person's progress, they also stopped working on their own side of the bridge, so the whole project stopped.

For the project to work, Sally and Ted must understand that they each work differently, and trust that neither way is the only way to do it. Both ways are equally important and necessary for the project to work out.

2) "Mandy" and "Joe" are married. Mandy has two part time jobs, loves to take on several new projects around the house, has children from a previous marriage, is in a book club, a knitting club, and a women's group, and often volunteers at her spiritual community. Joe is a photographer, has no children of his own, works out at the gym with his friends a few times a week, and goes to a bowling league twice a month. Both partners enjoy their time together as well as the things they do on their own, both lead busy lives, and both of their lives are very different. Joe is used to doing things consistently and steadily, and prefers to move into new things slowly. Mandy is used to doing many new things all the time and enjoys filling her down time with more projects.

One day, Mandy decides she wants Joe to get involved in some of her projects, and when she asks him, Joe politely says, "no thanks, I have a lot going on today." Mandy becomes frustrated and she puts some things on Joe's to-do list since, it seemed to her, he wasn't working on anything. Joe becomes angry and asks Mandy to stop putting her things on his list. He even tells her, "Maybe you should chill out on doing so many different projects. I think you are doing too much, and it is stressing me out." Mandy tells him, "but you aren't doing anything, and I could use some help around here."

Joe and Mandy have started trying to build each other's side of the bridge. Just because it looks like Joe isn't doing something doesn't mean he isn't. And just because Mandy is so busy all of the time doesn't mean she is overwhelmed.

When individuals or groups work on their own side of the bridge, it will eventually get built (if it is meant to). When the time comes to create the middle section of the bridge- teamwork, cooperation, and a good deal of trust- will bring the two sides together.

Some things to remember when building a bridge with another person or group:

A) When you need help, you must ask for it.

B) If it looks like the other person needs help, simply ask them if they need help instead of assuming they do.

C) Every person works at a different pace, in a different rhythm, and with different tools. Notice how the pace, rhythm, and tools another person uses are generally "just right" for that person, the same way yours are generally "just right" for you.

D) Create tools and ways to cooperate when you meet the other person/people in the middle of the bridge you are building together.

E) It may be helpful to remember that your side of the bridge and their side of the bridge are still the same bridge (you are on the same team and working toward the same goals).

For the next few days, find ways to notice and recognize if you are trying to work on another person's side of the bridge. When you catch yourself, take a moment to pause, breathe, and simply ask them if they need help. And if you notice someone is trying to work on your side of the bridge and you don't want them to, pause, breathe, and gently let them know, "I am doing fine and do not need help right now, thank you; I will be sure to ask for help when I need it."

Remember, in relationship with others you are often working toward the same (or similar) goals. Do your best to find the common place in the middle of your goals with others while maintaining your side and trusting they will maintain theirs. TRUST is the key word here!

4) Life Visioning

Visioning is a great tool to support you in knowing the highest potential for yourself to allow what you desire into your life. Visioning is different from visualization, manifesting, vision boards, or basic meditation. While experience with any or all of those other visualization tools may be *helpful* in integrating Life Visioning into your life practice, it is not necessary to have knowledge of them for visioning to work. Along with doing daily "gratitude and seed planting" (p. 77), Life Visioning is one of my favorite tools to use for my personal growth and evolution.

The Life Visioning tool was created and developed in the early 2000's by Rev. Michael Bernard Beckwith, founder and spiritual director of the Agape International Spiritual Center in southern California. You can find several videos of Rev. Beckwith explaining visioning on YouTube. Search for: "Michael Beckwith Life Visioning Introduction."

To best explain the concept of visioning here, I will quote Michael Beckwith himself from an article he wrote at *essence.com/ 2012/ 03/ 22/ are-you-living-up-to-your-highest-potential/*

"The Life Visioning Process is a non-sectarian, universal spiritual technology which empowers us to live our highest potential in our eight life structures, including: ego, beliefs, relationships, livelihood, finances, health, spirituality, and community. When practicing Life Visioning, we place ourselves in contact with the unique blueprint of our own soul and download the Spirit's vision for our life (which some might call 'the will of God')."

Prior to taking an eight-week visioning course at my Centers for Spiritual Living (CSL) community, I was focused on using vision boards and visualization to create my life and manifest my goals and desires. While I still love using those tools, I have found they can be somewhat time consuming, and often lack the quality I can get from using Life Visioning. Visioning allows a larger perspective than my individual mind can conceive, and I am able to release what I think I want out of a situation to a more *Universal* idea that wants to come to life *through* me for myself, others, and the greater whole.

An example of this is: Following through on things to completion used to be a difficult issue for me. I could have created a vision board and posted on it reminders (pictures, sayings, quotes, etc.) of how to get better at completing things, or I could have meditated on my idea of completing tasks. Instead, knowing how to use Visioning, I decided to go through the process and listen for "God's idea" or the "Higher knowing" of what I needed to allow to guide, support, and energize me. After about 20-30 minutes, the awareness of God's idea for me was MUCH clearer than what I "thought" I should do. Any time I think I know what I need, or need to do, I understand that there is a higher knowing, or larger vision for me than I can possibly contemplate by myself, and Visioning is a way to tune into that vision. Every day now, I am getting better and better at following through and completing things! I know this is due to the information and awareness that came to me through the Life Visioning Process.

Along with the Life Visioning book and classes, Dr. Beckwith also created a system called the "Life Visioning Kit" which includes CDs, a book, and cards that teach you an immediate way to align your life (and what you choose to see and experience in it) with the ultimate Source of creation.

For more information about visioning, Agape, or Michael Beckwith, you can do an online search for "Michael Beckwith," "Life Visioning," or "Spiritual Visioning Process," or simply go to *agapelive.com*.

5) <u>GTG (Go To Gratitude)</u>

In the Egg Stage, I mentioned in the "Gratitude" tool (p. 51) that "gratitude will eventually be what you turn to during crucial moments in your life." Go-To Gratitude (GTG) is a tool that embodies this concept.

Write down and memorize two or three of your favorite things you are grateful for. It could be a memory of an occasion in your life that brought you much joy, a family member, pet or friend, an image of your favorite thing in nature, etc. That way, if anything stressful comes up, you now have two or three Gratitudes to "go to" for support in centering yourself and dealing with the situation in a calmer and more relaxed manner.

I have found that if stress shows up out of the blue, or something happens to cause pain, fear, or old patterns to surface, it is always best to have my "Go-To Gratitudes" close at hand. When I can go to gratitude during any uncomfortable situation, I immediately find that my breathing slows down, my focus becomes more relaxed, and the stress, fear or pain moves toward a more manageable level, often disappearing.

Even if a seemingly negative situation comes up, there is always good in your life. When you can remember that, and your GTGs, you can become adept at dealing with whatever stress comes up instead of pushing it away or pretending it doesn't exist.

"Cultivate the habit of being grateful for every good thing that comes to you, and to give thanks continuously. And because all things have contributed to your advancement, you should include all things in your gratitude."
~ Ralph Waldo Emerson

6) <u>Gathering Your Tools</u>

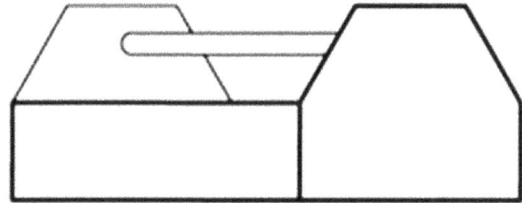

Remember everything you have learned through this book. Pull out some of your favorite tools and keep them in your memory, or write them down and keep them in your pocket or purse. Tell your friends about them, and ask them to remind you about them if you are feeling stuck.

Always remember, YOU are the creator of your life. You are the ONLY person in your life that can choose how you will live. When you let others make choices for you, it is still *you* who is choosing to allow it. There is no one to blame, no past bad memory you cannot heal and grow from once you choose to. You are the only one who can ask for help for yourself and allow it. If you are feeling stuck, scared, lonely, stupid, silly, hurt, frustrated, *you* have to be willing to look at yourself in the mirror and decide to move through it.

Use your toolbox! You are filling it up for now and for *future* use. Create new tools, use old ones, add to the old ones, mix new and old ... just USE them. Sharing a rich, powerful collection of spiritual tools is why I decided to write this book, and probably why you chose to read it and to work through it. So keep doing your work, use your tools, and allow yourself to be supported through all of your transformational times.

Butterfly Stage Conclusion:

The most important things to remember from this stage are: **Live for THIS moment, and be completely honest, authentic, and willing to move through your fears.**

This is *your* life; you get to *choose* how to experience it. You are the only person responsible for everything that happens in your life. At any moment, you have a choice and you have the power to change your circumstances. Life does not happen *to* you. It happens *through* you and *for* you.

You are the *only* person who can give yourself permission to claim, embrace, allow, and accept your life the way you choose to live it and experience it. If things seem to be falling apart around you, go through this book again and decide which stage of The Butterfly Process you are in. Read that chapter, journal, use the tools from that stage, and then move through the rest of the book until you find yourself here again.

Please be sure to read the Butterfly Process Conclusion on p. 133.

JOURNAL SECTION - Butterfly Stage

Beautiful Monarch of my Heart, your soft wings enfold me and hold me close, gently encouraging my own wings to unfurl, displaying hidden beauty.

~Michael Doss

Butterfly Process Conclusion:

Wherever you might be in your life, you are moving through some form of transformation, change, growth, or evolution. Any time you feel challenged by your life experiences and are ready to take the next step into your evolution, remember this book and your toolbox. Whether you create your own tools, adopt any of the tools in this book, or borrow tools from other people, you are always creating your *own* "Tools for Transformation."

Listen to your inner guidance and follow your gut instincts. Your intuition is so much stronger (and smarter!) than your ego or any of those old pain-bodies. You are always being taken care of and guided to that which you are creating for yourself. No matter what it is, *you* are creating it. You can support your life by noticing all of the positive things happening in it. What you focus on grows. Plant and tend to those things you want more of in your life. I believe in you and I love you. I wrote this book for you! Continue to create your perfect "now," one moment at a time—and remember to **enjoy** your journey!

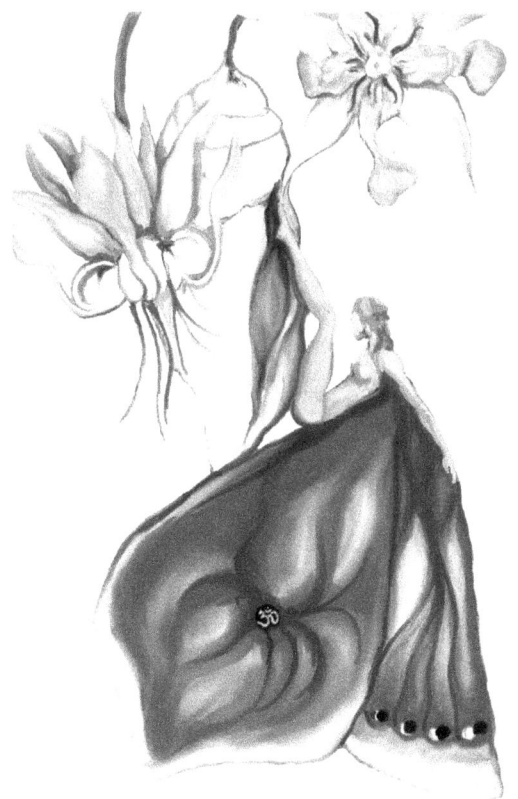

Postscript

I *really* wanted this book to fly, and near the end of the writing process, I started forcing myself to make it happen more quickly. Eventually, I realized I had to take an honest look at what I was writing about, and how I was not taking my own advice! I was pushing to "make" this book happen without allowing the time and patience it needed to be completed in its *own* time.

This is a perfect example of how to use (and not use) *The Butterfly Process*. I was going crazy trying to force myself to find images and pictures to use in the book, and trying to get permission to use them from people I do not even know.

After some toil and trials, I worked through my own Butterfly Process and finally realized I needed to *ask for help*! I also realized I could draw some of the images *myself*! I opened up to my inner artist and discovered something new about myself that I now deeply embrace and enjoy.

To all of the artists and poets who contributed to this book, I love you, and I thank you! With your help, this book was able to truly emerge from its cocoon and FLY. I am SO GRATEFUL to each and every one of you!

Artist and Poet Information

Below, I have listed each artist/poet in alphabetical order by last name, and the page(s) where their artwork/poetry is presented.

- **Laura "Leela Vox" Alexander**:
  One for ONE at 1:00- p. 95
  Web: *lifewithleela.com*
  Email: *leelavox@mac.com*

- **Stasia Bliss**: *"Self" poem-* p. 143
  Web: *facebook.com/stasiabliss.author*
  Email: *stasiabliss@gmail.com*

- **Terra Bundance**: *Big Butterfly-* pp. 9, 149; *Chakra Person-* p. 20; *Corral Diagrams-* pp. 35-41; *'Self' Image-* p. 42; *Life's Purpose-* p. 44; *Eggs on Leaf 1-* pp. 54, 139; *Eggs on Leaf 2-* p. 57; *Assemblage Point Image-* p. 64; *Notes-* p. 67; *Enneagram-* p. 71; *Caterpillar Out of Egg-* p. 81, 140; *Cocoon 1-* p. 103; *Cocoon 2-* p. 105, 141; *Bridge-* p. 119; *"Canvas" poem-* p. 153
  Web: *terrabundance.com*
  Email: *terraoutloud@gmail.com*

- **Leo Cortez**: *Butterflies-* pp. 6, 18, 19, 27, 109, 114, 131, 142, 145, 147, 150, 152, 155, 157, 159, 161, 163; *Toolboxes-* pp. 28, 52, 62, 89, 115, 127; *Corrals-* pp. 34, 43; *Bathtub-* pp. 45, 94; *Group Meditation-* p. 47; *Hearts-* p. 53; *Wishing Caterpillar-* p. 59; *Caterpillar Dreaming-* p. 78; *Drummers-* p. 91; *Sweat Lodge-* p. 99; *Free Butterfly-* p. 107 & 158; *Present/Gift-* p. 117; *Butterfly Mandala-* p. 164
  Web: *art-hero.com*
  Email: *leo@art-hero.com*

- **Michael Doss**: *"Monarch" poem-* p. 129
  Email: *shineyourlifellc@gmail.com*
  Web: *www.shineyourlifellc.com*

- **Sharon Farmer**: *Butterfly Life Cycle*- p. 15; *Egg Cycle*- p. 22; *Caterpillar Cycle*- p. 58; *Cocoon Cycle*- p. 84; *Butterfly Cycle*- p. 108; *Spiral Butterfly*- p. 128
  Web: *facebook.com/SherryFarmerArtist*
  Email: *sherryEFThealing@bellsouth.net*

- **Connie Mink**: *Meditating Open Heart*- pp. 46, 92
  Web: *goinghappy.com* / conniemink.com
  Email: *conniemink@gmail.com*

- **Christine Ruddy**: *"Fly!" poem*- p. 12; *"Caterpillar At Rest" Poem*, p. 79
  Web: *facebook.com/wordofspiritpoetry*
  Email: *ruddy.christine@gmail.com*

- **Léo Washburn**: *Butterfly Emerging*- cover art *and p. 2 & 133*
  Email: *imleo9@gmail.com*

- **Mary (Last name withheld)** (Age 8 at the time of creation): *Cute Butterfly*- p. 112

- **Jordan (Last name withheld)** (Age 10 at the time of creation): *Spiral Heart*- p. 30; *Journal*- p. 32

All images and poems are owned and copyrighted by Terra Bundance or the artist and cannot be used without written permission.

For permission, more information, or to find more from the creative artists, contact them through their emails or websites above. (You can contact the two younger contributors through Terra.)

Explanations of Terms

1) <u>Pain-Body</u> (pp. 16, 26, 33, 111, 133): *"Any negative emotion that is not fully faced and seen for what it is in the moment it arises does not completely dissolve. It leaves behind a remnant of pain. It may show up later as anxiety, anger, outbursts of violence, [moodiness], or even as a physical illness. These old, negative energies form an energy field that lives in the very cells of your body and is known as the pain-body"* (Eckhart Tolle, *A New Earth*, pp. 141, 142).

2) <u>Inner Guidance</u> (p. 24): Intuition, instinct, gut feeling, heart calling, the "Big Yes."

3) <u>EFT</u> (p. 33): Emotional Freedom Technique, also known as Tapping. *"Although based on the principles of acupuncture, EFT has simplified the realignment process by gently tapping on key meridian points on the head, torso and hands to help rebalance the body's energy system with respect to unresolved emotional issues. Energy meridians that run through our body can be blocked or disrupted by unresolved emotional issues, thereby compromising our natural healing potential. Realigning the energy meridians while focusing on an unresolved emotional issue can often provide increased personal peace and relief from many physical symptoms"* (Gary Craig, who popularized and made EFT known to the general public, *eftuniverse.com*)

4) <u>Law Of Attraction</u> (p. 49): *"Simply put, the law of attraction is the ability to attract into our lives whatever it is we desire. In basic terms, all thoughts turn into things"* (*thelawofattraction.com*).

5) <u>Imaginal Disks/Cells</u> (p. 85): *"One of the clusters of undifferentiated cells [just under the epidermis of] the larvae and pupae of some insects from which the wings, legs, and other organs of the adult are formed"* (Source: *m-w.com*).

"Masses of hypodermic cells carried by the larvae of some insects after leaving the egg from which masses wings and legs of the adult are subsequently formed"

(Source: *thefreedictionary.com*).

More detailed information on Imaginal Cells/ Disks:

- *todayifoundout.com/index.php/2011/10/caterpillars-melt-almost-completely-before-growing-into-butterflies-in-the-chrysalis/*
- *ravenessences.wordpress.com/2010/08/17/caterpillar-to-butterfly-via-imaginal-disks*
- *learner.org/jnorth/tm/monarch/chrysalisdevelopmentLPB.html*

Toolbox Summary:

You can add your own tool names here for each stage, and even journal about them in the Journal section on pp. 143-164

From the Egg Stage

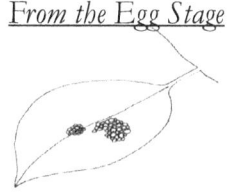

1) Taking Responsibility (p. 29)
2) Heart-Centered Breathing (p. 30)
3) Journaling (p. 31)
4) Emotional Freedom Technique (EFT) (p. 33)
5) The Corral exercise (p. 34)
6) Cleansing/clearing baths or showers (relaxing and being very gentle with yourself) (p. 45)
7) Meditation (p. 46)
8) Yoga (p. 47)
9) Supportive Groups and Individuals (p. 48)
10) Your Intention for Food, Water, Other Life-Energy (p. 49)
11) Acceptance (p. 50)
12) Gratitude (p. 51)
13) Creating Your Own Tools (p. 52)

From the Caterpillar Stage

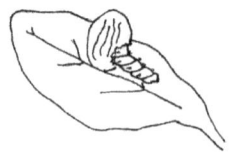

1) Explore High-Heart Chakra/Assemblage Point (p. 63)
2) Discover Inspiration (Books, Music, Quotes, Stories, Movies, Speakers, etc.) (p. 66)
3) Trying Something New (Toastmaster, Choir, Classes, Workshops, Writing Clubs, Group Outdoor Activity, etc) (p. 69)
4) Challenging Yourself (Step Out of Comfort Zones) (p. 70)
5) Explore The Enneagram (p. 71)
6) Notice Synchronicities/"Coincidences" (p. 72)
7) Gratitude and Planting Seeds (p. 77)

From the Cocoon Stage

1) Attend Nurturing Retreats or Workshops (Quiet Time, Relaxation, Rest, Meditation, etc.) (p. 90)
2) Get a Massage, Acupuncture, or Other Energy Work (p. 92)
3) Watch Nurturing Movies (p. 93)
4) Take Integrative Baths (Simple, Silent) (p. 94)
5) Practice "One for One at 1:00" Daily (p. 95)
6) Do a Fast and/or Cleanse (p. 96)
7) Practice Feng Shui, Clearing Your Environment (p. 97)
8) Consult Divination Cards (p. 98)
9) Participate in Shaman-Led Experiences (Sweat Lodge, Soul Retrieval, Journeying) (p. 99)
10) Keep a Gratitude and Dream Journal (p. 101)

From the Butterfly Stage:

1) Create a Healthy Lifestyle (Food Intake and Water, Exercise, Care by Health Practitioners, etc.) (p. 116)
2) Live in the Moment, Be Present (p. 117)
3) Explore "Building Bridges" (p. 119)
4) Practice Life Visioning (p. 124)
5) "GTG" (Go To Gratitude!) (p. 126)
6) Gather Your Tools (Quick Reference For Future Use) (p. 127)

MAIN JOURNAL

Self ... show me how to grow, let my feelings show, open up and know that what I have is all worth loving; all my dreams are more than nothing. Empower me from the core... oh self of mine, oh spirit free, embrace me with the reality of loving everything I do, living a life that's really true, authentically – only me.

I'm ready to be.

Oh, lead me carefully! Self.

~Stasia Bliss

Crying and laughing as life spills out in front of me
like paint being thrust on a canvas around me.
I am the rain, the wind, the stars and the sun. I am the canvas
and I am the paint, I am the painter and I am the paintbrush.
Whatever comes or goes is what is meant to be.
I am the creator of the life I see!

~Terra Bundance

www.ingramcontent.com/pod-product-compliance
Lightning Source LLC
Chambersburg PA
CBHW062109080426
42734CB00012B/2802